NORTH MACEDONIA

TRAVEL GUIDE

2023

The Ultimate Guide to exploring North Macedonia, adventure, discover the culture and explore the great sights and hidden gems of North Macedonia

Christopher Levell

Copyright

Table Of Contents

INTRODUCTION

Here you can find the 2023 Travel Guide for North Macedonia. This book attempts to provide you with all the necessary details and insider knowledge you need to make the most of your trip to this stunning Balkan nation.

You may find intriguing information about the country's geography, long history, cultural heritage, demography, and governance in the "About North Macedonia" section. You'll develop a greater respect for the nation and its citizens if you comprehend these features.

We can help you with your trip plans to North Macedonia. If you're coming by air, land, or sea, find out about the admission procedures and visa information, as well as the several modes of transportation that are available. Additionally, you may learn about the country's regional transit options and the ideal season for travel based on the climate and upcoming festivals. We also provide linguistic insights into North Macedonia and communication advice to help you communicate with locals more effectively.

We go over practical topics like currency and money conversion in the "Essential Travel Information" section to make sure you're ready for financial transactions while traveling. We also provide helpful health and safety advice, such as any vaccines or safety measures that may be required. To protect yourself and your possessions, don't forget to think about purchasing travel insurance. Finally, to respect North Macedonia's culture and traditions, get to know the regional manners and customs.

Our guide will help you arrange your schedule whether you want to visit the energetic capital city of Skopje, the peaceful beaches of Lake Ohrid, or off-the-beaten-path locations. Learn about the must-see sights, distinctive outdoor pursuits, cultural experiences, and lively celebrations that capture the heart of the nation. Discover the finest restaurants to satiate your cravings for fine dining while indulging in the tastes of Macedonian cuisine, including traditional meals and regional delicacies.

We'll provide helpful tips on where to stay, how to get about North Macedonia and provide cultural and linguistic insights throughout the book. We'll also talk about crucial health and safety issues, such as how to get emergency services and where to find medical facilities.

We've included a variety of helpful tools to improve your trip experience, including suggested maps and guidebooks as well as tourist information centers and online travel services. Also included in our appendix are conversion tables, helpful idioms, a dictionary of regional words, and an index for quick access.

Prepare to set off on a fascinating adventure across North Macedonia, where you will encounter ancient history, breathtaking scenery, friendly people, and delectable food. As you discover the wonders of this magical nation, let this book serve as your reliable travel companion.

About North Macedonia

Landlocked North Macedonia, often referred to as the Republic of North Macedonia, is a nation on Southeast Europe's Balkan Peninsula. In the northwest, it borders Kosovo; in the north, Serbia; in the east, Bulgaria; in the south, Greece; and in the west, Albania.

This multicultural nation is well known for its extensive history, gorgeous natural surroundings, and lively cultural heritage. Its crucial geographic position at the confluence of Europe, Asia, and Africa has had a long-lasting impact on its history and culture.

The history of North Macedonia, which reaches back to antiquity, is intriguing. It was once a part of the Roman Empire before rising to prominence during the Byzantine and Ottoman Empires. It was a part of Yugoslavia up until it became independent in 1991 in more recent times.

The nation is proud of its rich cultural past, which was influenced by several civilizations, including the Illyrians, Romans, Byzantines, Ottomans, and Slavic peoples. Its customs, food, music, and architecture all exhibit this fusion of elements.

The capital and biggest city of North Macedonia, Skopje, is a bustling center with a blend of contemporary and traditional features. It has a diverse collection of modern, neoclassical, and Ottoman-era buildings among other architectural styles. The city is renowned for its robust nightlife, several museums, and busy bazaars.

The gorgeous scenery of North Macedonia will charm nature enthusiasts. Beautiful mountain ranges in the nation, such as the Ar Mountains and the Mavrovo National Park, provide chances for hiking, skiing, and other outdoor pursuits. Lake Ohrid, a UNESCO World Heritage site renowned for its crystal-clear waters and abundant wildlife, is one of the nation's most valued assets.

The inhabitants of North Macedonia are well recognized for their kind hospitality and open arms. Although Albanian and other minority languages are frequently used, Macedonian is the official language. Although there are sizable Muslim and other religious groups, the Eastern Orthodox Christian religion is practiced by the majority of the people.

North Macedonia is a multi-party democratic parliamentary republic. With a recent emphasis on economic growth, tourist marketing, and integration into international organizations, the nation has achieved great progress.

North Macedonia provides an enthralling travel experience, whether you want to explore the historical sites in Skopje, immerse yourself in the cultural legacy of Ohrid, or take in the natural beauty of the countryside. Each visitor will get a lasting image of this nation because of its fascinating history, breathtaking scenery, and kind people.

Making a trip to North Macedonia

North Macedonia travel is a thrilling experience, and the information in this part will help you organize your trip successfully.

Information about entry requirements and visas:

Make sure you are aware of your country's visa requirements well in advance.
Ascertain if you need a visa or whether you qualify for admission without a visa.
Make sure your passport is valid for at least six months after the day you want to travel.
Learn the processes for entering and leaving at seaports, land borders, and airports.

Options for transportation

- **By Air**: The primary international entry point is Skopje International Airport (SKP). A minor airport is Ohrid St. Paul the Apostle Airport (OHD), for example.

- **By Land**: If coming from a nearby country, take into account using the bus, rail, or vehicle. Make sure you have the required paperwork, such as a global driver's license or a border crossing permit.

- **By Sea**: There are a few ferry services available for travel from neighboring nations.

North Macedonia's Local Transportation:

- **Public transportation**: The main forms of public transportation, providing connectivity to several cities and areas around the nation, are buses and railroads.

- **Taxis**: You may hail a taxi on the street or using a smartphone app, and they are widely accessible in metropolitan areas.

Renting a vehicle offers flexibility and makes exploring North Macedonia simple. Make sure you have the proper insurance and driver's license.

Ideal Season to Visit

The climate of North Macedonia is continental, with hot summers and chilly winters.

There are fewer people and beautiful weather throughout the spring (April to June) and fall (September to October) seasons.

Although it might become busy, summer (July and August) is a popular time to explore Lake Ohrid.

In mountainous areas, winter (December to February) is the best time for skiing and other winter activities.

Communication via Language:

Macedonian is the official language. However, English is a common language in resort areas, hotels, and dining establishments.
For communicating with locals, learning a few fundamental Macedonian words and phrases or having a phrasebook might be useful.

Before traveling to North Macedonia, it is advised to read the most recent travel warnings and speak with your local embassy or consulate for the most recent details on entrance procedures and safety precautions.

Important Travel Advice

There are a few important things to bear in mind before coming to North Macedonia. This section goes over key elements to guarantee a hassle-free and pleasurable journey.

Exchange of money and currency:

The Macedonian Denar (MKD) is the country of North Macedonia's official currency.
Banks, exchange offices, and a few hotels provide currency exchange services. Urban regions have a large number of ATMs that accept the most popular foreign debit and credit cards.

Tips for health and safety

Having travel insurance that pays for medical costs, including emergency evacuation, is advised.

Before departing for North Macedonia, confirm any prescribed immunizations with your doctor.
Bring copies of your prescriptions and any required medicines.

Consistently take safeguards for your protection, such as paying attention to your surroundings and locking up your things.

Travel Protection:

Having travel insurance that covers unexpected medical expenses, trip cancellation or interruption, and loss or theft of personal possessions is strongly advised.

Examine the policy's specifics to make sure it addresses all of your demands and anticipated actions.

Etiquette and customs

- When visiting religious places, observe clothing standards and other regional norms.

- Handshake everyone you meet and make eye contact all the time.
- When entering a house, it's polite to take your shoes off.
- Tipping is commonly accepted, particularly in restaurants and for excellent service.

Important Contact Info:

- Keep a list of emergency phone numbers, including those for the local police, ambulance, and fire departments.
- Make a note of the North Macedonian embassy or consulate's phone number.
- Before and throughout your journey, it is crucial to remain up to speed on any travel warnings or updates issued by your government or other relevant agencies.

  Traveling in North Macedonia will be safer and more pleasurable if you abide by local rules and ordinances.

II. PREPARING FOR YOUR TRIP

Visa and Travel Documents

It's essential to comprehend the necessary travel paperwork and visa requirements before making travel arrangements to North Macedonia. To aid you in making the necessary preparations, this section offers an overview.

Passport Requirements

Make sure your passport is valid for at least six months after the day you want to travel.
Verify that your passport includes empty pages for stamping entries and exits.
Before your vacation, think about renewing your passport if it is about to expire.

Visa Requirements

Examine your country's visa requirements well in advance of your trip.

Many nations may enter North Macedonia without a visa, and visits there can last up to 90 days during a 180-day term.

Even for brief stays, certain nations may need a visa or entrance authorization. Check the particular criteria for the nation where you now live.

Application for a Visa:

If a visa is essential, get acquainted with the application procedure and acquire all relevant paperwork.

For comprehensive information on visas and the application process, get in touch with the North Macedonian embassy or consulate closest to you.

Give yourself enough time to complete your visa since it can take a few weeks.
Other required paperwork:

You could be required to provide supporting documentation in addition to a current passport and visa, like:
A letter of invitation from the host or a hotel reservation serves as evidence of accommodations.
Evidence of adequate cash, such as bank statements or a letter from your company, is required to pay for your stay.
Flights that are round-trip or continue.

Border Checkpoints:

Know the precise border crossing points' locations and opening times.
Learn about the entrance and departure processes, including the criteria for immigration and customs.
The most up-to-date visa and entrance requirements must be confirmed via official sources, such as the North Macedonian

Ministry of Foreign Affairs or the closest embassy or consulate. To make sure you have a trouble-free trip to North Macedonia, plan and prepare your travel papers well in advance.

Safety and Health Measures

When visiting North Macedonia, it's important to adopt appropriate hygiene and safety precautions. This section offers crucial advice and safety measures to guarantee secure and healthy travel.

Travel Protection:

- Invest in comprehensive travel insurance that includes evacuation and emergency medical coverage.
- Verify that any planned activities, such as hiking or adventure sports, are covered by your insurance policy.

Medical Resources:

Learn the locations of the pharmacies, medical facilities, and hospitals in the places you'll be visiting.

- Make sure you know how to reach emergency medical care.
- If you need to take any particular drugs, pack enough for the length of your vacation.

Vaccinations:

- To find out whether any vaccines are advised for travel to North Macedonia, speak with your doctor or a travel clinic.
- Make sure any standard vaccines, such as those for influenza, diphtheria, pertussis, tetanus, measles, mumps, and rubella, are up to date.

Warnings for your health:

- Use filtered water to consume and wash your teeth, particularly in rural regions, or purchase bottled water.

- Maintain excellent hygiene habits by using hand sanitiser or washing your hands often with soap and water.
- Be mindful of food safety and only eat food that has been adequately prepared from trusted sources.

- Use insect repellent and wear proper clothes to avoid being bitten by insects, particularly while engaging in outside activities.

Safety measures:

- Use reliable sources to stay up to date on the state of security and safety both before and during your trip.

- Take safety measures to protect your possessions, such as locking up valuables and being mindful of your surroundings.
- Respect cultural sensitivity and local laws and traditions.

- Utilize trustworthy modes of transportation, and exercise caution while crossing roadways.

Emergency numbers:

- Make a note of the local police, medical services, and the embassy or consulate of your country in North Macedonia.
- Put these phone numbers into your phone's contact list for quick access.

It's always good to keep up with travel warnings and abide by any advice given by your government or other relevant authorities. You may have a safe and fun day touring North Macedonia by adopting the required health and safety measures.

Packing List

It's crucial to prepare thoughtfully for your trip to North Macedonia and to take your itinerary's particular requirements into account. To make sure you have everything you need, here is a recommended packing list:

Clothing:

- Lightweight, comfortable clothing that is appropriate for the weather (for example, t-shirts, shorts, and skirts in the summer; long-sleeved shirts, slacks, and layers in the winter).
- If you want to explore the outdoors or hike trails, use sturdy walking shoes or hiking boots.
- If you want to visit lakes or swimming pools, bring swimwear and a towel.
- a thin sweater or jacket for chilly nights at higher altitudes.
- For sun protection, use a hat, sunglasses, and sunscreen.

Travel necessities:

- A current passport and all required visas.
- Your trip documentation (passport, visa, tickets, and hotel bookings), either printed or digital.
- Information about travel insurance as well as emergency contacts.

- Power converters and adapters for Type C and Type F sockets in North Macedonia.
- For on-the-go charging of electrical gadgets, use a portable charger or power bank.
- a reliable daypack for hiking or day outings.

Safety and Health:

- prescribed drugs and copies of the prescriptions.
- Basic first aid kit containing all the necessary supplies, including sticky bandages, painkillers, disinfectant wipes, and any personal prescriptions.

- To guard against mosquitoes and other biting insects, use insect repellent.
- For on-the-go hygiene, use wet wipes or hand sanitiser.

Communications and electronics:

- Phone and charger for it.
- Use a camera or a smartphone to record special occasions.
- Use a mobile Wi-Fi gadget or a local SIM card to access the internet.
- headphones or earbuds for listening to music

Miscellaneous Items:

- Maps or travel guides are used as references.
- Eye mask and a travel cushion for a nice night's sleep when traveling.

- reusable travel bottles or travel-sized amenities (toothbrush, toothpaste, shampoo, etc.).
- For locking your bags, use a travel lock.
- Depending on the season, a lightweight rain jacket or an umbrella.
- Never forget to check the weather forecast for the time you will be traveling and pack appropriately. For day trips and excursions, it's a good idea to pack a small bag with the necessary items. Consider any specific activities or occasions you intend to attend before packing (such as hiking gear or formal attire for formal occasions).

Prioritize your essentials and think about using the laundry facilities or services at your accommodation if you want to travel light. You may have everything you need while keeping your baggage reasonable and practical by packing thoughtfully.

Money and Currency Issues

It's crucial to manage your finances and understand the local currency when visiting North Macedonia. Here is some crucial information about money and currency:

Currency:

The Macedonian Denar (MKD) is the country of North Macedonia's official currency. λ
- 100 deni make up one denar, the unit of currency.
- Coins: There are coins with the denominations of 1, 2, 5, 10, and 50 denis as well as 1, 2, 5, 10, and 50 denari.
- Banknotes: There are banknotes with denominations of 10, 50, 100, 200, 500, 1000, and 2000 dinars.

Converting Money:

In major cities and popular tourist destinations, banks, exchange offices, and some hotels offer currency exchange services.
To ensure you are getting the best deal possible, compare fees and exchange rates.

When you arrive, it's a good idea to exchange enough money for your immediate needs.

Visa and MasterCard:

Urban areas have a large number of ATMs that accept the most popular international debit and credit cards.
To prevent any problems using your credit card abroad, let your bank or credit card company know about your travel plans.
Check your bank's ATM fees and withdrawal restrictions.

Money Usage

Although most hotels, restaurants, and bigger institutions take credit cards, it is advisable to have extra cash on hand for smaller stores, markets, and rural locations where cash may be preferred.
Make sure you have small amounts on hand for ease of use, particularly when paying for transportation or items in neigneighbourhoodkets.

Security and Safety:

Take the appropriate safeguards to protect your assets and money.

When traveling, think about wearing a money belt or carrying a concealed bag to carry your cash and critical papers.

Keep a note of your card data, including contact numbers for reporting lost or stolen cards.

Tipping:

Tipping is not mandatory in North Macedonia, however, it is traditional to round up or offer a little tip for excellent service in restaurants, cafés, and taxis.

Check whether a service fee is already included in the statement before adding an extra tip.

It's usually a good idea to carry a range of payment choices, including cash and cards, for flexibility and ease. Monitor exchange rates and be careful while handling cash to prevent scams or counterfeit currencies. By being conscious of currency and money problems, you may assure a seamless financial experience throughout your vacation to North Macedonia.

Language and Communication

When visiting North Macedonia, mastering the language and communication customs may substantially improve your experience. Here's some vital information to help you handle language difficulties and communicate effectively:

- **Official Language:**

The official language of North Macedonia is Macedonian.
Macedonian employs the Cyrillic character, therefore acquaint yourself with the alphabet to understand signs and basic information.

- **English Proficiency:**

English is extensively spoken in tourist areas, hotels, restaurants, and stores, particularly in bigger towns like Skopje and Ohrid.
However, competence levels may differ among people, therefore it's helpful to learn a few fundamental words in Macedonian.

- **Basic Phrases:**

Learning a few easy Macedonian words may be beneficial and appreciated by locals. The following are some keywords:
Greetings: драво (Zdravo)
In appreciation: лаодарм (Blagodaram)
Yes: Да (Da)
No: Не (Ne)
е молам (Ve molam), kindly
I apologize: винете (Izvinete)
овидувае (Voveduvanje): Goodbye

- **Language Resources:**

To facilitate conversation, carry a phrasebook or utilize smartphone language translation applications.
Apps for offline translation are helpful when there is restricted internet connectivity.
Cultural Manners:

It's polite to extend a handshake and make eye contact while speaking with natives.

Using "please" and "thank you" is crucial since in Macedonian society, respect and politeness are highly prized.

When attending places of worship, dress modestly and adhere to any prevailing traditions or rules.

- **Directions and Symbols:**

Major cities often use both Latin and Cyrillic characters for their street signs and other public transit signage.

To read signs, maps, and transit information, it is helpful to have a rudimentary comprehension of Cyrillic lettering.

- **Centers fCentresist Information:**

For help with maps, brochures, and other language-related questions, go to the local tourist information offices.

English-speaking staff members who may provide advice on attractions, travel options, and lodging may work at these facilities.

Remember that even if you just use a few basic words, the locals will appreciate your effort.

Respect and an openness to learning may lead to fruitful encounters and improve your trip to North Macedonia.

Regional traditions and manners

Understanding regional traditions and etiquette is essential while visiting North Macedonia to respect the local way of life and interact amicably with the populace. To remember, have the following in mind:

- **Greetings and decorum**

Handshake everyone you meet and make eye contact all the time.
Address people using formal titles and last names, particularly in formal contexts.
It is usual to say "Hello" with "драво" (Zdravo) and "Goodbye" with "овидување" (Voveduvanje).

- **Fashion Code**:

When visiting places of worship like churches and monasteries, dress modestly. Women should cover their shoulders and refrain from donning shorts or other provocative attire.
Casual dress is often suitable in more relaxed environments, such as restaurants or cafés.

- **Observing customs and traditions:**

When visiting religious places, show respect by adhering to any regulations or instructions, such as taking off your shoes or covering your head.
Before shooting pictures of people or in certain settings, especially in rural regions, be sure you have their permission.

- **Dining Manners:**

It's normal to send a little gift, like flowers or chocolates, for the host when you're welcomed to someone's house.
Table manners are comparable to those in other European nations, such as avoiding putting your elbows on the table and keeping your hands visible throughout meals.

To express gratitude for the dinner, it is customary to eat everything on your plate.

- **Tipping:**

Although not required in North Macedonia, tips are appreciated for excellent service. If you are happy with the service, it is typical to tip 5–10% of the total cost in restaurants.
Rounding up the fee in taxis is a regular practice.

- **Personal Space and Body Language:**

When talking with natives, respect their personal space and refrain from approaching too closely.
Impolite gestures include pointing with your finger or your foot. Instead, identify directions or things using an extended hand motion.

- **Communication and Socializing:**

The Macedonian way of life emphasizes friendliness and sociability. Engage in cordial conversation and gladly accept invites.

Be a good listener and demonstrate an interest in discovering the customs and culture of the area.

Subjects like politics or history should be avoided until they spontaneously come up in conversation.

You may foster healthy connections and make a favorable impression on the people you encounter while visiting North Macedonia by exhibiting respect for the regional customs and traditions.

III. GETTING TO KNOW NORTH MACEDONIA

A. Geography and climate

Planning your journey requires an understanding of North Macedonia's topography and climate. An outline of the topography of the nation and the normal climate you might anticipate is given in this section:

- **Geography:**

The southeast European nation of North Macedonia is a landlocked member of the Balkan Peninsula.
Kosovo, Serbia, Bulgaria, Greece, and Albania all border it.

The nation is renowned for having a wide variety of topography, including mountains, lakes, valleys, and undulating hills.

The mountain range known as the Ar Mountains, which stretches over the western portion of the nation, is the most notable geographical feature.

- **Climate**:

The climate of North Macedonia is transitional, with influences from both the Mediterranean and the continent.
Depending on the location, summers (June to August) are often hot and dry, with average temperatures ranging from 25°C to 35°C (77°F to 95°F).

The coldest months are winter (December to February), with average temperatures ranging from -5°C to 5°C (23°F to 41°F), especially at higher altitudes.
The months of spring (March to May) and fall (September to November) may be enjoyable travel times because of the warm weather.
Regional Differences:

There are noticeable climatic variances across North Macedonia as a result of differences in height and geographic factors.

The winter months are often colder and snowfall is frequent in mountainous areas, such as the Mavrovo National Park and the Pelister National Park, providing chances for winter sports.

In contrast to the hilly areas, the southern portions of the nation, including the city of Bitola, have milder winters and warmer summers.

- **Precipitation**:

The spring and autumn seasons are when the nation receives the most rain.

Usually dry and with little precipitation, summers.

various geographical locations may see various patterns of precipitation, with larger quantities in mountainous regions and lower totals in the country's eastern sections.

Consider the region's unique climate while making your travel arrangements, and pack appropriately. Remember that weather conditions might change, so it's best to check the forecast closer to the day of your trip. North Macedonia's varied environment has plenty to offer any tourist, whether they enjoy outdoor activities in the mountains or discovering cultural landmarks in cities.

B. Culture and History

Your trip experience will be enhanced and you will get vital insights into North Macedonia's history and culture. A summary of North Macedonia's history and culture may be found here:

- **History**:

The area that is now North Macedonia has a long history that dates back to the ancient era. The Roman, Byzantine, and Ottoman Empires, among others, all had a presence there.

Ottoman Rule: From the early 20th century until the middle of the 14th century, North

Macedonia was governed by the Ottoman Empire.

Balkan Wars and the Yugoslav Period: Following the Balkan Wars at the beginning of the 20th century, Serbia ruled the area. Subsequently, it was included in the Socialist Federal Republic of Yugoslavia.

After Yugoslavia's disintegration, North Macedonia proclaimed its independence in 1991. The Federal Republic of Yugoslavia, from which the State Union of Serbia and Montenegro eventually emerged, originally included it. It finally changed its name to the Republic of North Macedonia in 2001.

Historical Culture:

- **Ethnic Diversity**: The people of North Macedonia are from a variety of ethnic backgrounds. The main ethnic groups are, among others, Turks, Romanis, Macedonians, and Albanians.

- **Traditional Arts and Crafts:** The nation has a long history of producing traditional arts and crafts, such as woodcarving, ceramics, filigree jewelry, and textiles.

- **Cuisine**: Balkan, Mediterranean, and Turkish cuisines all have an impact on North Macedonian cooking. Kebabs, ajvar (roasted pepper spread), graves (baked beans), and different cheeses are examples of popular foods.

- **Folklore and Festivals**: Traditional music and folklore are significant components of North Macedonian culture. Traditional music, dancing, and attire are shown during festivals like the Vevani Carnival and the Ohrid Summer Festival.

- **Eastern Orthodox Christianity**: is practiced by the majority of people in North Macedonia. But there are also sizable Catholic and Muslim populations.

C. Cities and Regions

Each area and city in North Macedonia has its special attractions and experiences. Here are some noteworthy areas and cities to visit:

1. Skopje

Skopje, the nation's capital, is a lively metropolitan area with a mix of traditional and contemporary attractions. Here are some Skopje highlights:

- **Kale:** Explore the historic fortification in Skopje, Kale, which is perched on a hill above the city. It has sweeping views over Skopje and is home to several artifacts from antiquity.

- **Stone Bridge:** This bridge, which crosses the Vardar River and links the ancient and modern areas of the city, is a well-known emblem of Skopje. It provides a relaxing stroll over the river and is decorated with statuary.

- **Experience the vibrant atmosphere of the Old Bazaar:**, a historic bazaar from the Ottoman period, in Stara Arija. Explore the stores, cafés, and traditional crafts that line its winding lanes.

- **Macedonia area:** the main area of Skopje, Macedonian area (Makedonija), is decorated with fountains and monuments, including a large statue of Alexander the Great riding a horse. It is a well-liked gathering spot and meeting location.

- **Mother Teresa** : Visit Mother Teresa Memorial House to see where the Nobel Peace Prize winner and well-known humanitarian was born. Her life and efforts are celebrated in the memorial home via exhibitions and relics.

- **Museum of Contemporary art**: Explore modern and contemporary art at the Museum of Contemporary Art, which has an amazing collection of pieces by Macedonian and foreign artists.

- **Skopje City Museum**: Explore exhibits from the prehistoric era to the present to learn about Skopje's history and culture.

- **Vodno Mountain**: Take a cable car or a stroll to the massive cross located on Vodno Mountain, the Millennium Cross. From the summit, take in the panoramic views of Skopje.

During your trip to North Macedonia, Skopje is an interesting place to see since it provides a variety of historical sites, cultural attractions, and a dynamic cityscape.

2. Ohrid

Ohrid, a charming city in the southwest of North Macedonia, is well-known for its scenic lake, ancient attractions, and natural beauty. Here are some of Ohrid's highlights:

- **Explore Ohrid Lake**: one of Europe's oldest and deepest lakes, which is renowned for its pristine waters and stunning surroundings. Enjoy water sports like swimming and boating or just unwind by the lake.

- **Ohrid Old Town**: Explore the quaint, cobblestone lanes of this UNESCO World Heritage Site. Explore the traditional stores, take in the beautifully preserved medieval buildings, and pause at neineighbourhoodfés.

- **Church of St. Sophia**: Admire the magnificent Byzantine architecture of this historic building, which dates to the eleventh century. Its bell tower provides sweeping views of the city and the lake and has beautiful paintings.

- **The little chapel known as St. John at Kaneo:** which is perched on a rock above Ohrid Lake, is a well-known representation of Ohrid. Enjoy stunning views of the lake and the mountains in the area.

- **Samuel's Fortification**: Explore the remains of Samuel's fortification, a mountaintop fortification erected in the tenth century, by ascending to it. You can get panoramic views of Ohrid and the lake from the castle walls.

- **Hellenistic era** :Visit the impressively preserved historic theater from the Hellenistic era in Ohrid. Attend concerts and cultural activities held in this historic space.

- **Platonik Archaeological**: Visit the Platonik Archaeological Site to see the ruins of the Church of St. Clement and an early Christian basilica. The location also has a museum and St. Clement University.

- **Icon Gallery:** Take a tour through the Church of St. Sophia's Icon Gallery. Observe an extensive collection of religious icons, some of which date back to the 11th century.

- **Bay of Bones Museum:** the extraordinary Museum of Water in the Bay of Bones Museum, which is perched above Lake Ohrid. It displays art artifacts on the early history of the area as well as replicas of ancient pile houses.

- **Boat Tours**: Take a boat excursion on Ohrid Lake to explore the new neighborhood top at remote beaches, and take in picturesque lake and mountain vistas.

Ohrid is a must-visit location for tourists looking for somewhere to unwind and go exploring because of its stunning natural surroundings, fascinating history, and cultural heritage.

3. Bitola

Bitola is a medieval city with a fascinating ambience and a rich cultural history that is situated in the southwest of North Macedonia. Here are some of Bitola's highlights:

- **Shirok Sokak**: Walk along Shirok Sokak, a pedestrian boulevard dotted with neoclassical structures, cafés, stores, and eateries. In Bitola, it is a bustling and well-liked meeting spot.

- **Explore the colorful tara area" or "Old Bazaar"**: in Bitola to take in the busy atmosphere, peruse the local wares, and sav regional specialities

- **Visit the Heraclea Lyncestis** : to learn more about this ancient city that Philip II of Macedon established. Inverell-maintained remains, which include Roman baths, baths, and mosaic flooring.

- **Admire the magnificent Yeni Mosque**: which was constructed during the Ottoman period. It is a well-known landmark in Bitola due to its exquisite construction and elaborate embellishments.

- **The Bitola Clock Tower** : may be climbed for panoramic views of the city and its surroundings. Enjoy the beautiful views and take some lasting pictures.

- **Visit the Isak Mosque**: a gorgeous Ottoman mosque with a tranquil courtyard and beautiful architecture. It is one of North Macedonia's biggest mosques.

- **Bitola Museum**: Located in a former military academy, the Bitola Museum offers information about the history and culture of Bitola. The museum displays a variety of historical objects.

- **Explore the adjacent Pelister National Park**: which is renowned for its clean environment and stunning vistas. Hike through thick woods, find alpine lakes, and take in breathtaking mountain top vistas.

- **Experience the splendor of the Old Turkish Bazaar**: which is close to the Yeni Mosque. It provides a window into Bitola's Ottoman history and is a fantastic location to purchase handicrafts and souvenirs made locally.

- **Dragor River**: The city's central river may be explored by taking a roll along its banks. Enjoy the beautiful scenery and peaceful environment.

Bitola is a wonderful location for examining North Macedonia's cultural legacy because of its blend of history, architecture, and natural settings.

4. Tetovo

The city of Tetovo is situated in North Macedonia's northwest. It is renowned for its energetic vibe, ethnic variety, and iconic buildings. Here are some of Tetovo's highlights:

- **Visit the well-known Painted Mosque (arena Damija)**: which is noted for its beautiful facade decorated with brilliant floral and geometric motifs. It is a wonderful illustration of Islamic artwork and construction.

- **Explore the 16th-century complex** : This consists of a mosque, a tomb, and other structures at Arabati Baba Tekke. It serves as a significant spiritual and cultural hub for the Sufi Bektashi order.

- **Tetovo Fortress**: Learn about the remnants of the Tetovo Fortress, which are positioned on a hill above the city. It provides sweeping views of Tetovo and the mountains around it.

- **Pena Park:** Take a legal spot in this tranquil green haven with lovely scenery, trees, and trails. It's the ideal location to unwind and escape the bustle of the city.

- **Visit the National Gallery of Macedonia:** in Tetovo to see famous Macedonian painters' creations on display. It features exhibits of a range of artistic disciplines, such as painting, sculpture, and photography.

- **Explore Tetovo's Old Town (Varo**) : to see its quaint streets and classic homes. Visit tiny businesses, take in the atmosphere, and Macedonian food at neighborhood eateries.

- **Tetovo Market**: Take in the vibrant mb-ambience of this market where you can buy a range of fresh foods, regional crafts, and traditional Macedonian goods.

- **Arabati Baba Music Days**: If you go to the country in July, you may be able to attend the Arabati Baba Music Days, a music event that will include performances by well-known musicians from North Macedonia and the Balkan area.

- **Shar Mountain**: Explore the surrounding area's natural enjoying outdoor pursuits including mountain biking, skiing, and hiking. Explore the unspoiled countryside while taking in the breath-blowing sights.

Tetovo is renowned for its cultural variety and has a sizable Albanian community. Experience the combination of Macedonian and Albanian culture, food, and music while embracing the cosmopolitan atmosphere.

Tetovo provides tourists with a distinctive and educational experience in North Macedonia by blending cultural, historical, and natural features.

5. Prilep

The medieval city of Prilep, which is situated in the southwest of North Macedonia, is well-known for its tobacco industry, historic landmarks, and scenic surroundings. Here are some of Prilep's highlights:

- **Visit the famous King Marko's Tower**: a stronghold from the Middle Ages perched on a hill overlooking Prilep. Explore the ruins while taking in the expansive views of the city and the surroundings.

- **Varosh Old Quarter**: Take a trip around Prilep's historic Varosh district. Observe the classic architecture, the congested streets, and the old homes with exquisite stone carvings.

- **Monastery of Treskavec**: Take a tour of this tranquil and attractive medieval monastery situated on Mount Zlato's slopes. It provides breathtaking vistas, historic frescoes, and a serene setting.

- **Prilep Museum**: Visit the Prilep Museum to learn more about the city's rich history and cultural heritage. It has a variety of exhibitions, including artwork, ethnographic objects, and archaeological relics.

- **Visit Marble Lake (Prilepsko Ezero)**: a tiny man made lake surrounded by stunning scenery, which is close by. It's a well-liked location for picnics, fishing, and taking in the tranquil scenery.

- **Explore the Zrze Monastery**: a nearby medieval monastery renowned for its stunning paintings and peaceful environment. It is tucked away in a stunning natural environment.

- **Tobacco Museum**: Visit the Tobacco Museum to learn about Prilep's past as a major tobacco manufacturing hub. Learn about the region's tobacco production, cultivation, and importance.

- **Kuklica Stone Dolls**: A short drive from Prilep, the Kuklica Stone Dolls are a rare example of a natural occurrence. These naturally occurring rock pillars, which exhibit human-like features, are well-liked tourist destinations. Visit the Markovi Kuli archaeological site, where you may see the remains of a bygone fortification a window into the area's extensive prehistoric past.

- **Pelagonia Folk Museum**: At the Pelagonia Folk Museum, you may learn about the traditions and traditional culture of the Pelagonia area. It showcases domestic products, crafts, and clothing from the local culture.

Prilep is a fascinating location for tourists interested in learning about North Macedonia's history and landscapes because of its blend of historical monuments, scenic landmarks, and cultural attractions.

6. Kratovo

Eastern North Macedonia's little town of Kratovo is renowned for its beautiful surroundings, well-preserved medieval buildings, and rich history. Here are some of Kratovo's highlights:

- **Stone Bridge:** Take a look at this charming medieval bridge that crosses the River Kratovska. It serves as the town's emblem and provides a picturesque location for pictures.

- **Visit the Church of St. Nicholas**: a breathtaking Orthodox building renowned for its magnificent paintings and tranquil ambience of the town's oldest churches is this one.

- **Explore the Kratovo Old Bazaar's** : winding lanes, which are dotted with classic homes, art galleries, and coffee shops. Investigate regional handicrafts while taking in the genuine environment.

- **Discover the subterranean tunnels** : This previously provided the town with a network for its water supply. Visit these distinctive and interesting tunnels on a guided tour.

- **Clock Tower**: For sweeping views of Kratovo and the hills around it, climb the clock tower in the town here, you can see the town's historic beauty in all its glory.

- **Visit the adjacent Kuklica Stone Dolls**: This is a unique natural phenomenon where rock formations mimic human beings. It is a distinctive and enigmatic attraction.

- **Explore the Markovi Kuli Fortress ruins**: which are situated on a hilltop with a view of Kratovo. Take in the sweeping vistas and consider their historical importance.

- **Ethnographic Museum**: Discover Kratovo and the area's customary culture and way of life at the ethnographic museum. It displays crafts, furniture, and clothing from the past.

- **Visit the Krttheo Carnival:** Take part in the exciting celebrations and vibrant parades of hohonouringhonourings' rich cultural history and customs.

With its natural splendor, laid-back ambience, and insight into North Macedonia's medieval past, Kratovo is a delightful vacation spot for history buffs and environment lovers.

7. Kumanovo

Northern North Macedonia's Kumanovo is a city renowned for its historical importance, cultural legacy, and scenic surroundings. Here are some of Kumanovo's highlights:

- **Visit the Goce Delev Memorial Museum:** learn more about this monument to the revolutionary and national hero of North Macedonia. Find more about his life, accomplishments, and battles for freedom.

- Explore the Kumanovo Old Bazaar, a bustling marketplace where you can discover regional goods, handmade crafts, and traditional Macedonian food. Take in the lively ambience and learn about the culture of the area.

- **Visit the. Nicholas's Church:** is a gorgeous Orthodox building with exquisite paintings and elaborate iconography. In Kumanovo, it is a major religious and cultural site.

- **Clock Tower**: For sweeping views of Kumanovo and its surroundings, climb the clock tower in the city and take breathtaking pictures.

- **Discover the ruins of Marko's Tower**: A castle from the Middle Ages that bore the name of the mythical hero King Marko. From the summit, explore the ruins and take in the beautiful scenery.

- **Visit the Kokino Observatory**: An old astral observatory and archaeological site, by taking a short excursion from Kumanovo. It provides a fascinating window into historical astronomy understanding.

- **Kumanovo City Museum**: Visit the Kumanovo City Museum to learn more about the city's history and cultural heritage. Learn about historical items, records, and exhibits that are related to the city.

- **Kumanovo Liberation Memorial**: Pay respects to the dead warriors and heroes of Kumanovo at this moment in honoring the region's liberation fights and conflicts.

- **Turtlemanovo Jazz**: Enjoy live performances by local and international jazz musicians if you go to Turtlemanovo Jazz Festival. Discover the city's thriving music scene and cultural events.

- **Outdoor Activities:** Take part in outdoor activities including hiking, bicycling, and nature walks to have a better understanding of Kumanovo's natural surroundings. There are options for leisure and adventure in the adjacent mountains and sceneries.

North Macedonia's Kumanovo is a fascinating place to visit because of its historical sites, cultural monuments, and scenic surroundings.

8. Struga

Struga, a quaint village in the southwest of North Macedonia, is well-known for its lovely lake, literary legacy, and cultural events. Here are some of Struga's highlights:

- **Explore the breathtaking Lake Ohrid:** one of Europe's oldest and deepest lakes. Enjoy water sports, swimming, and sunbathing, or take a leisurely boat trip to take in the scenery and explore .

- **Struga Poetry Evenings**: Attend the famous Struga Poetry Evenings, an annual gathering of poets from across the world. It draws poets and authors from all around the globe as its nursery and literary works.

- **Ohrid Old Town**: Not far from Struga, Ohrid Old Town is a UNESCO World Heritage site. Discover its quaint streets, stop by its antique churches, and be amazed by its extensive cultural and historical legacy.

- **The renowned Bridge of Poetry**: which crosses the Black Drin River, must be crossed. Enjoy the tranquil ambience while seeing the stone reliefs that include poetry.

- **Visit the charming Kalishta Monastery:** which is located on Lake Ohrid's eastern bank. It offers a serene and spiritual experience with its beautiful paintings and cave churches.

- **Struga City Museum:** Visit the Struga City Museum to learn more about the city's history, culture, and customs. It shows ethnographic objects, archaeological displaysaboutwn's literary past.

- **Fishermen's Village:** Investigate the Fishermen's Village, which is situated beside the lake. Taste delicious fish meals, take in the tranquil surroundings, and learn about the local fishing culture.

- **Visit Cinar Square:** Struga's main square, by clicking here. With its cafés, restaurants, and stores, it is a bustling meeting area. Relax in one of the outside sitting areas while taking in the colorful colorful full

- **Discover the House of Robevci:** a historic structure that today functions as a museum and cultural history while admiring the architecture.

- **Struga Beaches**: The pebble and sand beaches along Lake Ohrid's shores are great places to relax. Take advantage of the sun, clean seas, and a variety of water sports.

Struga is a charming location for tourists looking for a mix of leisure and cultural discovery in North Macedonia because of its natural beauty, cultural activities, and literary legacy.

9. Gostivar

Gostivar, a bustling city in western North Macedonia, is renowned for its cosmopolitan culture, interesting historical landmarks, and active marketplaces. Here are some of Gostivar's high points:

- **Gostivar Bazaar**: Take a stroll through the vibrant, busy Gostivar Bazaar, where you can buy a wide range of products, including fresh food, spices, apparel, and handicrafts. Experience the local culture and immerse yourself in the lively environment.

- **Visit the Clock Tower**: a notable landmark in the heart of Gostivar. For sweeping views of the city and its surrounding at the end of the summit.

- **Isa Bey Mosque**: Take in the stunning architecture and elaborate embellishments of this mosque from the Ottoman period. It is among the area's oldest mosques.

- **Explore the Varos area**: which is the oldest section of Gostivar. Explore its winding streets, take in the charming old homes, and soak up the atmosphere.

- **Marko's Tower**: Explore the remnants of the medieval fortification bearing the same name as the fabled hero King Marko. Explore the location, which provides panoramic vistas and historical value.

- **Visit adjacent nature reserves** : like Bistra and Dlaboka, which provide chances for outdoor pursuits including hiking, picnicking, and taking in the area's natural splendor.

- **Cultural Events**: Attend the year-round cultural events held in Gostivar, including music festivals, ethnic dance performances, and religious ceremonies. These activities highlight the city's thriving cultural variety.

- **Visit the Hamam Museum**: a bathhouse from the Ottoman period that has been turned into exhibitions reflecting Gostivar's history, culture, and traditions.

- **Explore the Murat Bey Mosque**: another important mosque in Gostivar, which is renowned for its stunning architecture and historical importance.

- **Local Cuisine:** Enjoy Gostivar's rich gastronomic scene. delicacies like burek and have as well as typical Macedonian and Albanian cuisine.

Gostivar attracts tourists seeking to fully experience North Macedonia's rich cultural diversity because of its diverse history, historical sites, and bustling marketplaces.

10. Other Important Locations

In addition to the areas and cities already listed, North Macedonia is home to noteworthy locations. Here are a few examples:

- **Mavrovo National Park**: This park, which is located in the west of the nation, is renowned for its breathtaking scenery , lakes, and thick woods. It provides chances to go trekking, go skiing, and take in the local scenery.

- **Matka Canyon** : is a magnificent natural site that is close to Skopje. It has multiple caverns, a serene lake, and a steep gorge. The area's nearby medieval monasteries are open for visitors to explore, along with boat cruises and hiking paths.

- **The highest mountain in the nation:** Mount Pelister, is found in Pelister National Park, which is situated in the southwest of North Macedonia. The park's varied flora and wildlife, glacial lakes, and beautiful hiking routes are well-known features.

- **Explore the ancient city of Stobi**: a significant archaeological site that was active throughout the Roman and Byzantine eras. Investigate well-preserved ruin sites, such as the Asilican a, the trend mosaics.

- **Visit the Popova Kula Winery**: which is close to the town of Demir Kapija. Tainpart win-wins union nne-tasting sets, visit vineyards, and discover how wine is made in North Macedonia.

- **The tallest town in North Macedonia**: Krusevo is situated in the country's concert concentrated views of the mountains in the area. It is well-known for its lengthy history, classic-style buildings, and yearly cultural events.

- **Vodno Mountain**: Located just outside of Skopje, Vodno Mountain provides hikers and mountain bikers with the possibility to enjoy panoramic views of the city while they are out in the great outdoors. The Millennium Cross, a well-known landmark, is also situated on this peak.

- **Kokino Megalithic Observatory**: Take a tour of the over 3,800-year-old Kokino megalithic observatory. It is one of the world's oldest observatories and offers insights into prehistoric astronomical expertise.

- **Visit the Tikves Wine Region**: which is renowned for its vineyards and wineries. Visit wineries, sample the wines produced there, and research the area's winemaking history.

- **Pelagonia Valley:** Explore this picturesque region, which is known for its huge plains, productive farms, and quaint settlements. It is an agricultural area well-known for producing dairy goods, fruits, and vegetables.

These famous locations provide a wide variety of experiences, from taking in wine tasting and outdoor activities to seeing historical landmarks and natural marvels. They highlight the diversity and depth of North Macedonia's geographies, cultures, and histories.

IV. PLANNING YOUR ITINERARY

Recommended Timeframe

The amount of time you should spend in North Macedonia depends on the destinations you want to visit and the activities you want to undertake there. However, a recommended stay would be between 7 and 10 days to obtain a thorough understanding of the nation. In this amount of time, you may see Skopje, the country's capital, as well as Ohrid, Bitola, and Prilep. You can also engage in outdoor sports in parks like Mavrovo and Pelister.

The proposed durations for several popular places are broken down as follows:

- **2 to 3 days for Skopje**: Discover the city's historical sites, museums, and thriving bazaars.

- **Ohrid two to three days**: Discover its cultural and historical landmarks while touring the UNESCO-listed Ohrid Old Town and taking in the breathtaking Lake Ohrid.

- **Bitola a day or two**: Visit historic ruins, see the city's Ottoman architecture, and take in the laid-back atmosphere.

- **One day in Prilep**: Explore the historical sites, including the Treskavec Monastery and King Marko's Fortress.

- **1 to 2 days for Mavrovo National Park:** Enjoy outdoor pursuits like skiing and hiking while discovering the park's natural splendor.

- **1 to 2 days for Pelister National Park**: Visit the medieval town of Brajcino, hike to the top of Mount Pelister, and discover the park's plants and animals.

Allocate one to two days for each of the following additional locations: Kratovo, Kumanovo, and Struga.

Naturally, you may change the length depending on your tastes and the amount of time you have for your vacation. Consider adding a few additional days as well to allow for downtime, pleasant surprises, or day visits to neighboring sights.

Must-visit Attractions

Several must-see places in North Macedonia highlight the nation's rich cultural legacy, natural beauty, and historical importance. Here are a few of North Macedonia's must-see sights:

- **Skopje**: Explore the historic stronghold known as Skopje stronghold in the center of Skopje (Kale). Enjoy the city's sweeping vistas while learning about its historical significance.

- **Visit Lake Ohrid**: one of Europe's oldest and deepest lakes and a UNESCO World Heritage site. Enjoy the area's crystal-clear seas, the quaint town of Ohrid, and all of its historical and cultural landmarks.

- **Matka Canyon**: Matka Canyon, close to Skopje, is a natural wonder. Explore the amazing caverns, take a boat ride on the serene lake, and trek the canyon's beautiful pathways.

- **Church of St. John at Kaneo**: Take in the stunning views of Lake Ohrid from the Church of St. John at Kaneo, a famous medieval church. It is a must-see location due to its scenic surroundings and stunning architecture.

- **Visit the Ancient City of Heraclea Lyncestis**: which is close to Bitola, and go back in time. Discover the amphitheater, basilica, and mosaic floors of this ancient city as you tour its well-preserved remains.

- **Visit the Stobi Archaeological Site**: one of the most important ancient Roman cities in North Macedonia. Observe the spectacular mosaics, temples, and theaters among the well-preserved remains.

- **Explore Pelister National Park**: which is renowned for its breathtaking alpine scenery and abundant wildlife. Discover the glacial lakes on Mount

Pelister's peak while hiking there, and take in the abundant wildlife and plants.

- **Discover the Sveti Naum Monastery:** which is situated on the banks of Lake Ohrid. soak a boat trip to the neighboring springs, see the church's stunning Byzantine architecture, and soak in the tranquil surroundings.

- **Shirok Sokak**: the main pedestrian street in Bitola, is studded with cafés, stores, and ancient structures. Take a stroll along it. Enjoy the dynamic atmosphere of the city and its rich architectural and cultural history.

- **Visit Mavrovo National Park**: which is renowned for its imposing mountains, spotless lakes, and an abundance of animals. Take part in sports including skiing, hiking, and route exploration in the park.

These must-see locations provide a variety of experiences, from historical and cultural places to natural marvels, enabling you to learn more about North Macedonia's beauty and history.

Destinations Off-the-Beaten-Path

Several undiscovered jewels in North Macedonia provide one-of-a-kind experiences and the possibility to go to less well-known regions of the nation if you're looking for off-the-beaten-path locations. Here are a few places worth investigating that are off the beaten path:

- **Kruevo**: tallest town in North Macedonia, Kruevo is situated in the scare care provicerereathtaking views of the mountains in the area. It is well-known for its yearly paragliding contests and has a long history and traditional architecture.

- **Demir Kapija**: A little village famed for its wine production, Demir Kapija is located in the picturesque Vardar River Gorge. Visit local wineries, tour local vineyards, and partake in wine tastings while surrounded by beautiful scenery.

- **Kokino Megalithic Observatory**: Learn about the nearly 3,800-year-old Kokino megalithic observatory. It offers sweeping vistas from its hilltop location and sheds light on the area's ancient astrological customs.

- **Explore the tobacco fields around Prilep**: which are renowned for their beautiful scenery and important economic contribution to the region. Visit historical tobacco drying facilities and learn about tobacco farming to get insight into this significant business.

- **Visit the quaint town of Vevani**: which is tucked away in North Macedonia's southwest. Vevani, which is well-known for its classic architecture and exciting carnival events, provides a window into the people and way of life in the area.

- **Discover the medieval village of Kratovo**: known for its beautifully preserved Ottoman buildings and an elaborate network of tunnels under the town. Discover the town's mining history as you stroll among the classic homes and stone bridges.

- **Mokra Gora**: A remote mountainous location in the Mavrovo region, Mokra Gora is renowned for its pure environment, charming settlements, and hiking paths. Immerse yourself in rural life, take in the peacefulness of the countryside, and engage in outdoor sports.

- **Stenje Waterfall:** Set off on an expedition to Stenje Waterfall, a secret paradise buried away in North Macedonia's western region. This magnificent waterfall provides a tranquil, unspoiled natural scene that is ideal for photographers and wildlife enthusiasts.

- **Mariovo**: Take a tour of the distant and thinly inhabited Mariovo region, which is renowned for its rocky scenery, stone settlements, and fascinating mythology. Discover the region's cultural legacy while hiking through beautiful scenery and experiencing the local way of life.

- **Visit the Prespa Lakes**: which are shared by North Macedonia, Albania, and Greece. These lesser-known lakes provide peace, possibilities for birding, and the possibility to find out-of-the-way communities and monastery ruins.

Away from the busier tourist regions, these off-the-beaten-path locations provide an opportunity to discover North Macedonia's hidden gems. They provide fascinating cultural encounters, breathtaking natural beauty, and a window into the nation's rich legacy.

Outdoor Recreation

A superb location for outdoor lovers, North Macedonia offers a variety of activities among breathtaking natural scenery. Here are some well-liked outdoor activities you may partake in, whether you want to go hiking, skiing, or participating in water sports:

- **Trekking & Hiking**: Discover North Macedonia's many hiking paths, including those in parks like Mavrovo, Pelister, and Galichica. Learn about the beautiful mountain views, the pristine lakes, and the varied flora and animals.

- **Snowboarding and skiing:** Visit ski destinations like Mavrovo, Popova Sapka, and Kozuf during the winter to hit the slopes. Enjoy winter activities like skiing and snowboarding while surrounded by stunning alpine scenery.

- **Water Sports**: Enjoy the nation's lakes and rivers for your favorite water sport. Enjoy water sports on Lake Ohrid, Lake Prespa, or the Vardar River, including swimming, kayaking, canoeing, and paddleboarding.

- **Experience the rush of paragliding over North Macedonia's stunning surroundings**: The Balkans' paragliding hub, Kruevo, is noted for its outstanding conditions and breathtaking scenery.

- **Rock Climbing:** Practice your climbing techniques on the cliffs and rock formations in places like Demir Kapija, Matka Canyon, and Mavrovo National Park. For climbers of all experience levels, these places provide a range of routes.

- **Mountain biking**: Take to the roads to explore North Macedonia's scenic landscape. Discover mountain riding routes in national parks or enjoy cycling through rural regions while admiring the beautiful scenery.

- **The Vrelo Cave in Matka Canyon and the Sharko Cave in Mavrovo National Park:** are two caves in North Macedonia that are worth investigating. Visit a spelunking site and be amazed by the marvels there.

- **Rafting**: Set out on an exhilarating rafting excursion on the Radika River, next to Mavrovo National Park, or the Treska River, close to Matka Canyon. As you go through the rapids, savor the thrill of excitement.

- **Camping and nature retreats**: Set up camp in one of the many beautiful places in the nation, from the highlands of Pelister National Park to the beaches of Lake Ohrid. Enjoy a tranquil getaway surrounded by the outdoors.

- **Animals watching**: A wide variety of animals, including bears, wolves, lynxes, and several bird species, may be found in North Macedonia. Participate in narrated birding and wildlife trips to see and understand the local animals.

North Macedonia has a wide range of outdoor activities to suit all interests and ability levels, whether you want an exhilarating adventure or a relaxing study of nature. Take advantage of the nation's natural splendors while having exhilarating and unforgettable experiences.

Cultural encounters

North Macedonia is a nation with a rich cultural history that provides tourists with a wide range of distinctive cultural encounters. Enjoy these cultural events to fully immerse oneself in the local customs, music, art, and gastronomic delights:

- **Visit the traditional celebrations that highlight the nation's cultural history**: The exciting cultural events that take place all year long include the

Bitola Shakespeare Festival, the Skopje Jazz Festival, and the Ohrid Summer Festival.

- **Taste traditional delicacies from North Macedonia and indulge in local cuisine:** Experience the delectable grilled meats, savory pies like burek, crisp salads, and sweet treats like baklava. Try the native rakija, a fruit brandy that is well-known in the Balkan area.

- **Folklore & Traditional Dance**: Take in performances of traditional dances and music that are a reflection of the rich cultural heritage of the nation. Folk festivals are held in many cities and towns, where you may enjoy real music, costumes, and exciting dance performances.

- **Visit historical locations like the Old Bazaar in Skopje**: which provides a window into the nation's Ottoman history, to learn more about North

Macedonia's Ottoman legacy. Explore the mosques, hammams, and traditional artisan stores built during the Ottoman period.

- **Visit the country's famous monasteries**: which are important historical, cultural, and spiritual sites. The Sveti Naum Monastery, Treskavec Monastery, and St. Panteleimon Monastery in Ohrid are famous for their architectural and theological importance.

- **Visit local markets and workshops to learn about traditional crafts and artisanal techniques**: Handmade items that make for interesting mementoes include pottery, woodwork, traditional fabrics, and jewelry fashioned of filigree.

- **Ethnographic Museums**: Take a look around the nation's ethnographic museums, including the Museum of Bitola and the Museum of Macedonia in Skopje. The cultural history, customary attire, and way of life of the many ethnic communities in North Macedonia are shown in these museums.

- **Visit Neighborhood Villages**: Make a diversion to charming traditional villages including Mavrovo, Jane, and Vevani. Discover the rural way of life, get to know the people, and discover their traditions.

- **Seminars in Traditional Music and Dance:** Attend seminars in traditional music and dance to learn the melodies and dancing moves. It's a great way to enjoy yourself while getting to know the local culture.

Admire the ancient architecture of the nation, which includes magnificent monuments, structures from the Ottoman Empire, and medieval churches. Discover locations like the Mustafa Pasha Mosque in Skopje, the Stone Bridge in Skopje, and the Church of St. John at Kaneo in Ohrid.

The legacy, customs, and way of life of North Macedonia are better-understood thanks to these cultural encounters. They provide you with the chance to mingle with the populace, learn about the culture, and make enduring travel experiences.

Festivals and Events

Year-round celebrations of the nation's cultural, historical, and artistic heritage are held in North Macedonia via a range of events and festivals. In North Macedonia, the following festivals and events are noteworthy:

- **Ohrid Summer Festival (July–August):** This well-known festival is held in the picturesque city of Ohrid and has a varied schedule of music, dance, theater, and visual arts. Enjoy shows by regional and international performers in breathtaking outdoor locations.

Jazz fans shouldn't miss the Skopje Jazz Festival, which brings together renowned jazz artists from all over the globe, each October. Enjoy the genre-celebrating shows, jam sessions, and seminars.

- **The Bitola Shakespeare Festival (July–August) honors William Shakespeare's literary creations**: Watch productions of his plays on stage, go to lectures, and take part in workshops focused on Shakespeare's writing and theater.

- **Vevani Carnival (January):** Take in the vibrant Vevani Carnival, a yearly celebration occurring in the Vevani hamlet. Participate in the celebration, watch the exciting parades, and take in the distinctive masks, costumes, and folklore customs.

- **The greatest Macedonian films will be on display during the Macedonian Film Festival, which takes place in September**: Viewings of long-form, documentary, and short films provide perspectives on the regional film business.

- **Balkan Terror! Skopje (October):** Balkan Trafik, a celebration of Balkan music and culture! A dynamic event called Skopje brings together performers, musicians, and artists from the Balkan area. Participate in seminars, concerts, and cultural activities.

- **Prilep Carnival** :One of the oldest and most vibrant carnivals in North Macedonia is the Prilep Carnival, which takes place in May. Join in the celebration as people march through Prilep's streets while wearing ornate costumes and dancing.

- **The D Festival**: which celebrates contemporary dance, takes place in August and features cutting-edge dance performances by regional and worldwide performers. Enjoy seminars, experimental dance styles, and contemporary choreography.

- **Galicnik Wedding Festival (July)**: Take part in this one-of-a-kind event, which recreates a traditional wedding ceremony in the charming hamlet of Galicnik. Discover the vibrant celebrations, music, and traditions.

- **National Day Celebrations (September 8):** On September 8th, major cities all around the nation will host a variety of activities to mark North Macedonia's Independence Day, including concerts, cultural performances, and fireworks.

Experience the rich and interesting cultural traditions, arts, and events of North Macedonia via these occasions and festivals. Plan your trip to coincide with these festivities so that you may take in the colorful ambience of these occasions.

Food and beverage encounters

ChatGPT
The cuisine of North Macedonia has a rich history and a wide variety of tastes and traditional recipes. Here are some dining and drinking options you need to check out while there:

- **Enjoy traditional Macedonian food:** which is known for its wide selection of grilled meats, fresh vegetables, dairy products, and substantial stews. Try foods like (Macedonian-style pizza), ajvar (red pepper relish), and tav grave (baked beans).

- **Local Markets**: To enjoy the lively atmosphere and discover a broad variety of fresh produce, spices, cheeses, and traditional delights, visit local markets like Bit Pazar in Skopje or Ohrid Bazaar in Ohrid. Meet welcoming merchants and learn about regional ingredients.

- **Rakija tasting**: Take a sip of this iconic Balkan fruit brandy that is a staple of Macedonian drinking customs. For a chance to sample many variations of this potent and fragrant alcohol, visit nearby vineyards or rakija producers.

- **Wine tasting**: North Macedonia has a long history of producing a wide range of top-notch wines. Visit local vineyards to sample local grape varietals and discover the wine-making process in areas like Tikve, Povardarie, or the Vardar Valley.

- **Cooking classes**: Take a cooking class to learn from local chefs how to make authentic Macedonian meals. Learn how to prepare delicacies like komplet lepinja (a substantial morning dish), tarator (a cucumber yogurt soup), and sarma (stuffed cabbage rolls).

- **sweets with an Ottoman influence:** North Macedonia offers a delectable selection of sweets and pastries with an Ottoman influence. Try sweets like trundle (rolled pastry filled with sweet fillings), tulumba (fried dough soaked in syrup), and baklava (layered pastry with nuts and syrup).

- **Dairy products**: North Macedonia is renowned for its top-notch dairy products. Try some locally made cheeses like feta, kashkaval, and arena sol (colorful cheese), which go well with bread, salads, or just by themselves as a snack.

- **Traditional Tea and Coffee**: Learn about North Macedonia's tea and coffee drinking traditions. Enjoy a cup of Turkish coffee or a traditional herbal tea, such as chamomile () or mountain tea (ski aj), at one of the quaint cafés or tea shops.

- **Outdoor grilling** :Participate in the well-known custom of outdoor grilling, also known as mangal or Skara. Join locals for grilled meats, kebabs, and veggies in parks, gardens, or other outdoor settings. These meals are often served with light salads and bread.

- **Sweet Delights**: Don't pass up the chance to sample the sweet treats of North Macedonia. Enjoy delights like Turabian n(butter biscuits with almonds), halva (a sweet dessert made from tahini and sugar), and Tulum (fried dough soaked in syrup).

You may learn about North Macedonia's tastes and culinary traditions by participating in these food and beverage activities. Each encounter gives a different sense of the cuisine of the nation, from regional drinks to traditional foods.

Purchases and souvenirs

Many distinctive and locally produced goods are available in North Macedonia that are great for presents and souvenirs. Consider the following buying excursions and well-liked mementoes:

- **Hands Mementoes:** To find a variety of handmade goods, browse neighborhood markets, artisan stores, and boutiques. Look for hand-painted pottery, kilims, carpets, copperware, delicate filigree jewelry, and traditional fabrics like these.

- **Traditional Costumes & Embroidery:** Traditional costumes and embroidered fabrics from Macedonia are lovely and significant keepsakes. You may purchase embroidered aprons, shirts, and accessories that highlight the nation's diverse ethnic traditions.

- **Robust wine sector**: North Macedonia is renowned for having a robust wine sector. As a memento, take a bottle or two of Macedonian wine home. Vranec, Kratoshija, and Stanuina are a few common grape varieties.

- **Ajvar and Regional Spices**: Ajvar is a traditional Macedonian condiment made from delicious red peppers. Look for ajvar in jars to enjoy at home. To give your food a little Macedonian flavor, you can also discover a range of locally derived spices and seasonings.

- **Premium honey**: North Macedonia is well-known for its premium honey and honey products. Find various kinds of honey, such as wildflower, chestnut, and acacia honey, by perusing neighborhood markets and honey stores. Additionally, honey-based goods like beeswax candles and skincare products are available.

- **Handwoven Carpets and Rugs:** The complex patterns and expert workmanship of Macedonian carpets and rugs are highly regarded. Look for handmade rugs in a range of designs and sizes that are made of wool or silk.

Buying souvenir t-shirts, magnets, keychains, and other items decorated with flags, buildings, or other traditional themes is a great way to show your support for North Macedonia.

- **Traditional Musical Instruments**: If you like music, you may want to purchase a gajda (a bagpipe), a kaval (a flute), or a (a drum) from Macedonia. These instruments are not only lovely, but they also provide a window into the nation's musical history.

Invest in a set that comprises a classic cezve (coffee pot) and tiny coffee cups to enjoy the Macedonian coffee-drinking custom. It enables you to duplicate the atmosphere of consuming Turkish coffee at home.

- **Traditional Food:** To bring the flavor of North Macedonia home, stock up on regional foods like honey, ajvar, Macedonian wine, and spices. These things make interesting presents for foodies or delights for yourself.

Before buying commodities like honey or food products, remember to verify customs procedures and limits to make sure you may carry them back to your own country. You may bring back a bit of North Macedonian culture and travel experiences by purchasing regional goods and mementoes to support local entrepreneurs.

V. ACCOMMODATION OPTIONS

1. Inns and resorts

You may choose from a variety of hotels and resorts in North Macedonia to suit your travel needs and price range. Consider some of the following accommodations:

- **Luxurious Hotels**: North Macedonia is home to several opulent hotels with first-rate features, tasteful accommodations, and first-rate service. These hotels often have swimming pools, fine dining restaurants, and spa amenities. The Aleksandar Palace Hotel in Skopje, the Marriott Skopje, and the Hotel Tino in Ohrid are a few examples.

- **Boutique Hotels**: In North Macedonia, boutique hotels provide a more individualized and private experience.

These more intimate hotels often have distinctive furnishings, chic rooms, and attentive service. Look for quaint lodgings in old houses or beautiful settings, like Villa Vinea in Kratovo or Villa St. Sofija in Ohrid.

- **Mid-Range Hotels:** Several mid-range hotels provide cozy accommodations, cutting-edge facilities, and warm service at a more reasonable cost. These lodging options provide a practical starting point for discovering North Macedonia's highlights. Examples include the Hotel Millenium Palace in Bitola and the Hotel Hamburg in Skopje.

Consider staying in a guesthouse or bed & breakfast for a more private and comfortable stay. These lodgings often provide a cozy setting, individualized service, and home-cooked meals. Smaller towns like Mavrovo and Jane and rural regions are where they are most prevalent.

- **Resorts**: North Macedonia is home to several resorts that provide a variety of amenities and leisure activities. The best places to stay are resorts if you want to unwind or participate in leisure activities like spa treatments, golf, swimming, or outdoor excursions. Aleksandar Villa & Spa in Dojran and Granit Hotel & Spa in Ohrid are two instances.

Accommodations with breathtaking lake views are a great option if you're traveling to Ohrid or other lakeside locations. Many lodging options, including hotels and guesthouses, are located right on Lake Ohrid's shoreline, providing scenic views and convenient access to water sports.

- **Eco-Lodges**: For individuals who like the outdoors and are looking for environmentally friendly lodging, eco-lodges provide a distinctive experience. These lodges emphasize eco-friendly methods and are often situated in beautiful natural settings. Etno Selo Timcevski in Mavrovo National

Park and Green Zone Pelister in Bitola are two examples.

- **Hostels**: In large towns like Skopje and Ohrid, tourists on a tight budget may locate hostels. For budget backpackers and lone travelers, hostels provide public areas, shared or private rooms, and a social atmosphere.

Consider things like location, facilities, closeness to activities, and your budget while selecting lodgings. To assure availability, it is important to make reservations in advance, particularly during busy travel times.

B. Bed and Breakfasts

In North Macedonia, guesthouses and bed & breakfasts provide a lovely and private stay, often with a personal touch and friendly hospitality. Because they provide a warm and welcoming ambience, these accommodations are especially popular in rural regions and smaller towns. The following information is provided on guesthouses and B&Bs in North Macedonia:

- **Location**: In North Macedonia, guesthouses and bed and breakfasts may be found in several locales, including attractive villages, hilly areas, and ancient cities. They provide an opportunity to take in the country's scenic splendor and native culture.

- **Accommodations**: Because guesthouses and bed & breakfasts often only have a few rooms, guests may expect a more intimate and pleasant stay. Frequently well furnished and with the essentials, rooms. Others could use communal restrooms while others might have private ones.

- **Homemade Meals**: The chance to eat meals that have been prepared from scratch is one of the benefits of staying at a guesthouse or bed and breakfast. Many hosts provide breakfast as part of the stay, with a choice of meals produced at home or using ingredients from the surrounding area. On request, certain lodgings may additionally provide supplementary meals that include local delicacies.

- **Personalized Service**: Innkeepers at guesthouses and bed-and-breakfasts are renowned for their gracious hospitality and attentiveness to guests. They often provide ideas for neighboring sites, events, and food alternatives and are kind and knowledgeable about the neighborhood.

- **Cultural Immersion**: You may get fully immersed in the community's culture by staying in a guesthouse or bed & breakfast. The history and customs of the region may be discussed by hosts, offering a window into the way of life there. It's a fantastic chance to meet people and discover their cultures and traditions.

Guesthouses and bed and breakfasts are often located in peaceful and picturesque settings, such as rural areas, mountain valleys, or next to lakes and rivers. Away from the rush of city life, this provides a serene and relaxing refuge.

- **Personalized Experiences**: Many inns and bed and breakfasts provide extra services and activities based on their visitors' preferences. Activities like culinary courses, wine tastings, guided hiking or biking trips, and traditional craft workshops may fall under this category.

Guesthouses and bed & breakfasts often provide a more economical lodging choice in comparison to five-star hotels. They are affordable, especially for tourists looking for an original and genuine experience.

When selecting a guesthouse or bed & breakfast, take into account the area, facilities, evaluations from prior visitors, and the particular ambience you're looking for. To guarantee your chosen lodging, it is advised to make bookings in advance, particularly during busy travel times.

Hostels and inexpensive lodgings

Hostels and other low-cost lodging choices are available in North Macedonia for tourists on a budget without sacrificing comfort. These lodgings are geared toward budget visitors, lone travelers, and those seeking a social environment. The following information about hostels and low-cost lodging in North Macedonia:

- **Location**: Hostels and inexpensive lodging are available throughout the nation's largest cities, including Skopje and Ohrid, as well as in well-liked tourist locations. They often have convenient locations that provide quick access to restaurants, public transit, and attractions.

Hostels often provide dormitory-style rooms with common bathrooms. The bunk beds in these rooms allow for many guests, fostering a convivial atmosphere where visitors may mingle and exchange stories. For individuals who would like to have more privacy, private rooms can also be provided.

- **Common Areas:** Hostels provide communal facilities for guests to unwind, mingle, and make meals, including lounges, kitchens, and outdoor areas. These spaces often provide a welcoming and social environment that enables visitors to interact with other visitors from other countries.

Budget hotels may provide fewer amenities than high-end hotels, but they still provide necessities like free Wi-Fi, shared kitchens, lockers for guests' possessions, and laundry facilities. Additional amenities like bike rentals or planned activities could be offered by certain hostels.

- **Social Events and Activities**: To assist visitors to discover the region and meet other travelers, many hostels provide social events, bar crawls, or city tours. These activities provide a chance to take in North Macedonia's thriving nightlife, cultural events, and well-liked sites.

- **Local Tips and Information**: Staff members at hostels are often familiar with the neighborhood and may provide helpful advice and suggestions for surrounding sights, restaurants, and transportation. They may help in making travel arrangements or booking excursions.

Hostels and other low-cost lodgings provide reasonable prices, which makes them a popular choice for tourists on a limited budget. There according to Therding the loss of location, tons of amenities, and room type (private or dormitory). To ensure availability and attractive pricing, it is advised to make reservations in advance, particularly during the busiest travel times.

- **An environment that is Backpacker-Friendly**: Hostels and low-cost lodgings provide a friendly setting for independent and backpacking travelers. It's a fantastic chance to connect with like-minded people, exchange travel tales, and make new friends from across the globe.

When choosing a hostel or low-cost lodging, take into account elements like location, feedback from prior visitors, facilities offered, and the ambience that best meets your interests. A pleasant and trouble-free stay may be ensured by making reservations in advance and reviewing the cancellation conditions.

D. Authentic Hotel Experiences

North Macedonia has various unique lodging options that go beyond conventional hotels and make visits unforgettable. These choices enable visitors to fully experience the nation's natural splendor, culture and history. Here are a few examples of distinctive lodging opportunities in North Macedonia:

1. Staying in a classic village home will give you a taste of rural life. These homes have undergone renovations to provide pleasant lodging while retaining their original beauty. Village homes may be found in picturesque areas, letting you take in the quiet countryside and mimingleith people.

- **Accommodations in caves**: North Macedonia is home to several taverns that have been creatively transformed into lodging. These caverns, with their apartments cut into the rock formations, provide a unique experience. A feeling of adventure and a connection to the natural environment are provided by lodging in a cave.

2. Staying at eco-friendly lodges is a great way to promote sustainable travel. These lodgings have an emphasis on protecting the environment and providing eco-friendly practices, such as employing renewable energy sources and encouraging responsible tourism. They are often found in protected or natural reserves, where hiking, animal watching, and other outdoor activities are possible.

- **Glamping**: With glamping (glamorous camping), you may have the best of both worlds. These campgrounds have opulent tents or cottages with plush mattresses, private toilets, and sometimes even air conditioning. Glamping enables you to appreciate contemporary amenities while taking in the splendor of nature.

Stay at a historic structure or castle that has been transformed into a hotel or guesthouse. These lodgings provide a window into the rich architectural and historical legacy of the nation.

You may savor the distinctive atmosphere, discover historical details, and treat yourself to a little luxury.

On Lake Ohrid in the city of Ohrid, there are floating homes. These one-of-a-kind lodging options let you stay right on the water, offering expansive lake views and a peaceful environment. It's an unforgettable way to take in Lake Ohrid's beauty and the serenity of being near water.

- **Accommodations in wineries and vineyards**: A few wineries in North Macedonia provide lodging within their vines. You may stay in guest houses or cottages surrounded by vineyards to experience the wine-making process firsthand and take in the beautiful surroundings. For wine lovers or those looking for a tranquil rural setting, it's the ideal choice.

When thinking about unusual lodging options, it's crucial to do your homework and make reservations in advance since there could not be many options available. These choices often provide a more individualized and private stay, enabling you to make long-lasting memories of your trip to North Macedonia.

VI. TRANSPORTATION IN NORTH MACEDONIA

A. Navigation in Skopje

The North Macedonian nation's capital, Skopje, provides a range of ways to travel about. The standard modes of transportation in Skopje are as follows:

- **Public Buses**: Skopje has a sizable public bus system that travels across the city and its environs. The buses are run by JSP Skopje and provide a practical means of getting about the city. You may find the routes and timetables at bus stations or on the JSP Skopje website. Have some spare coins on hand for the bus fare.

- **Taxis:** You may either order a cab from a taxi company or hail one on the street in Skopje. Seek authorized taxis with a meter and a firm logo. Before setting off on your excursion, it is wise to get the driver's best estimate of the cost.

- **Uber and Bolt**: two well-known ride-sharing services, are available in Skopje. Their smartphone applications let you hail a ride and pay for it simultaneously. This choice offers ease and often has clear pricing.

- **Walking**: The city core of Skopje is very small, making it simple to navigate on foot. The Old Bazaar, Macedonia Square, and the Stone Bridge are just a few of the city's attractions that can all be reached by foot. You may explore the city at your speed and find hidden treasures by walking.

- **Bicycles**: Skopje has launched a Nextbike bike-sharing program. One of the many docking stations located all across the city is where you may hire a bike. Simply download the Nextbike app, sign up, and use the app to unlock a bike. A terrific way to discover the parks, riverfront walkways, and bike-friendly regions of Skopje is by bicycle.

- **Car Rental**: You may hire a car from several car rental companies in Skopje if you prefer the freedom of having your vehicle. With a vehicle, you may go at your speed and explore the city's environs. It's crucial to get acquainted with the area's parking restrictions and traffic laws.

Joining guided tours or getting a private guide might be a practical method to see Skopje. These tours often include transportation to the main attractions as well as an interesting commentary on the history and culture of the city.

It is advised to plan your routes while moving about Skopje, particularly during rush hours, to prevent traffic congestion. Take safety measures and pay attention to your things, especially in busy places.

B. Using the Public Transit

Taxis and buses make up the city's public transportation system in Skopje, offering easy and reasonably priced ways to move about. More details regarding Skopje's public transit are provided below:

- **Buses**: JSP Skopje has a sophisticated bus network in Skopje. Buses link different areas and important sites along a variety of routes that run across the city and its surroundings. In Skopje, buses are often the most popular form of public transit.

Tickets for buses may be bought at booths located close to bus stops or straight from the bus driver before boarding. Drivers may not give you precise change, so be sure to carry it with you.

- **Bus schedules:** You may get bus timetables at bus stops as well as route details and schedules on the JSP Skopje website or mobile application. Bus service normally runs from early in the morning until late at night, with a reduction in frequency on weekends and holidays.

- **Travel Advice**: Arrive at the bus stop a few minutes before the departure time to avoid missing the bus. Give yourself additional time for your travel since buses might sometimes be packed during peak hours.

- **Taxis**: Taxis are widely accessible in Skopje and are a practical mode of transportation, particularly for shorter trips or while carrying baggage. Taxis may be requested via taxi companies or hailed on the street.

Taxis with a visible corporate emblem and a taxi sign on the roof are those that are legally allowed to operate. To guarantee fair pricing, the cab should have a working meter.

- **Cab Fare**: In Skopje, fares are calculated by factoring in both the distance traveled and the amount of time spent in the cab.

On the meter, the fare is shown. It's a good idea to ask the driver for an estimate of the fee before setting off on your trip.

- **Services for sharing rides**: In Skopje, popular ride-sharing services like Uber and Bolt are available as an alternative to regular taxis. Through their smartphone applications, you can both schedule and pay for rides.

It's crucial to keep a watch on your possessions and be mindful of your surroundings while utilizing public transit in Skopje. It's a good idea to double-check bus timetables for any modifications or alterations, particularly around holidays or significant occasions.

Overall, Skopje's public transportation system provides a dependable and affordable option to get to the city and visit the city's major sites and attractions.

C. Car Rental

Exploring the city and its surroundings may be flexible and convenient with a vehicle rental in Skopje. When hiring a vehicle in Skopje, keep the following things in mind:

- **Rental businesses**: Several international and local automobile rental businesses in Skopje provide a variety of cars to fit a range of purposes and price points. Along with local businesses, Hertz, Avis, and Europcar are well-known international vehicle rental firms having locations in Skopje.

- **Requirements**: To hire a vehicle in Skopje, you normally need to fulfill , such as meeting the minimum age requirement (usually 21 or 25), having a valid driver's license, and having a credit card on hand to pay the security deposit. It's crucial to confirm the precise specifications of the rental agency you choose.

- **Advance Reservations**: To assure availability and get a better deal, it is advised to make your rental vehicle reservations well in advance, particularly during busy travel times. You may make a reservation directly with the rental agency or via online travel sites that also provide vehicle rental services.

- **Driving Permit**: North Macedonia normally accepts driver's licenses that were issued by nations that use the Latin alphabet. However, if your driver's license is not written in the Latin script, you may also need to get an International Driving Permit (IDP).

- **Insurance:** Collision damage waiver (CDW) and theft protection are two of the common insurance choices provided by car rental agencies. It's crucial to comprehend the coverage offered and, if necessary, take into account supplemental insurance. Check to see whether your credit card provides coverage for automobile rentals.

Before driving in Skopje, familiarize yourself with the local traffic laws and restrictions. Driving is done on the right side of the road in North Macedonia, and everyone in the vehicle must wear a seatbelt. To guarantee safe and legal driving, it is important to adhere to speed limits, road signs, and parking restrictions.

- **Parking**: Skopje has both paid and unpaid parking spaces. Paid parking areas are identified by signage, and utilizing neighboring kiosks or mobile parking applications requires buying a parking ticket. There may be limited free parking spots available, particularly in crowded regions.

- **Navigation**: Using a GPS device or smartphone navigation applications may help you travel about Skopje and find your way to your target locations. Make sure your navigation is accurate and get acquainted with the routes you want to travel.

You may go at your leisure and reach more rural locations or attractions outside of the city when you rent a vehicle in Skopje. To drive safely, obey the law where you are, and take into account the local driving conditions and infrastructure before you go.

D. Ride-Sharing Services and Taxis

In Skopje, several alternatives for public transportation make it simple and easy to navigate the city. What you should know about Skopje's taxis and ride-sharing services is as follows:

- **Taxis**: Accessibility: You can easily locate taxis in Skopje at authorized taxi stops or ring them up on the street.

Taxis with a visible corporate emblem and a taxi sign on the roof are those that are legally allowed to operate. These cabs are often more dependable and run lawfully.
Meters and fee: Licensed taxis have meters that determine the fee depending on the amount of

time and distance driven. After your trip, ask for a printed receipt and confirm that the meter is operating. The cost of a taxi in Skopje is fair, but it's a good idea to ask the driver for an estimate before getting in the car.

- **Taxi Apps**: A few taxi businesses in Skopje have   that let customers book, monitor, and pay for taxis. These applications are practical and often provide the projected fee upfront.

Uber and Bolt are two well-known ride-sharing services that are accessible in Skopje. You may register, request a ride, and download your smartphone applications.   Real-time monitoring, predicted rates, and possibilities for cashless payments are all provided by the applications.

- **Availability**: With a large network of drivers spread out around Skopje, ride-sharing services provide a handy and dependable transportation choice. However, depending on the time of day and demand, availability may change.

The following advice should be kept in mind while savoring taxis or ride-sharing services in Skopje:

- **Safety**: Double-check that the information of the car you input lines up with those on the app or the taxi identification. Note the driver's name and pictures that are shown on the app. When selecting a cab or ride-sharing service, trust your gut and employ common sense.
- **Communication**: In case there are any language hurdles, having the address or site name written down or stored on your phone might be useful. Learn some basic instructions in Macedonian, or if necessary, utilize translation software.

Taxis typically take cash as payment, however, some may also accept credit cards. Payment for ride-sharing services like Uber and Bolt is made via the app using your registered payment method, so there is no need for cash.

When you desire a more direct and private transportation option, both taxis and ride-sharing services are practical choices for moving about Skopje. Choose between the two alternatives after taking your preferences, spending limit, and availability into account.

VII. DINING AND CUISINE

A. Customary Macedonian Foods

The Balkan area has a strong taste and cultural effect on Macedonian food. You should try the following classic Macedonian dishes:

- **Tav Grave**: is a traditional meal from North Macedonia that combines slow-cooked beans—typically kidney beans—with a variety of ingredients, including paprika, onions, and garlic. It is often served as a major dish and frequently goes with rice or bread.

- **Condigent ajvar** : Red peppers, garlic, and olive oil are used to make the popular condiment ajvar. It has a deep, savory taste and is often used as a sauce for grilled meats and vegetables as well as a spread for bread.

- **Shopska Salad**: Made with chopped tomatoes, cucumbers, onions, and peppers, this light salad is finished with crumbled white cheese, usually feta or sirene. Olive oil is used to flavor it, and parsley is often used as a garnish. It is the ideal starter or side dish.

- **Pastrmajlija**: is a traditional bread from Macedonia that is topped with chunks of roasted, marinated meat, often pig. A variety of herbs and spices are used to flavor the meat, giving it a unique flavor. It is a speciality meal that is often eaten on holidays or other special occasions.

- **Sarma**: Sarma is a meal composed of cabbage leaves packed with a mixture of grains, different herbs, and spices, as well as ground meat (often a combination of beef and pig). The filled cabbage rolls are tenderized over a slow fire in a delicious tomato sauce.

- **Kebapi**: Also known as kebabs, are tiny, grilled sausages cooked from a combination of ground beef or lamb and seasoned with herbs and spices like paprika, cumin, and garlic. They are often served with onions, ajvar, and flatbread.

- **Pita**: There are many different varieties of the pastry known as pita. Burek, which is created with layers of thin, flaky pastry filled with cheese, pork, or spinach, is one well-known variant. Zelnik is another variety and it's loaded with veggies like cabbage. A popular meal called pita is eaten for breakfast or as a snack.

- **Rakija**: Although it is not a food, rakija is a traditional fruit brandy from Macedonia and is a significant component of the country's culinary legacy. It is often produced with grapes, plums, or other fruits and is used as a digestif or aperitif.

These are only a few typical Macedonian meals to give you an idea of the rich culinary history of the nation. Experience the culture and tastes of North Macedonia by investigating the local food.

Region-specific Specialties

The numerous regional specialities of North Macedonia are well-known for showcasing the distinctive culinary traditions of several regions. You should sample the following regional specialties:

- **Ohrid Trout (Ohridska):** The southwest region of North Macedonia's Ohrid Lake is renowned for its mouthwatering trout. Normally, this freshwater fish is grilled or fried and served with potatoes or veggies on the side. You must try it if you are in Ohrid.

- **The Pelagonia area:** is well known for its tasty peppers, known as Pelagonia peppers (Pelagonka Piperka). These long, thin peppers are often filled with different ingredients, such as cheese or meat, or pickled and served as a condiment. They give food a distinctive, sour flavor.

- **The Bitola area**: is known for its substantial casserole dish known as Makedonska Tava (Macedonian Casserole). Potatoes, onions, peppers, tomatoes, and meat—typically pig or veal—are all included in it. It is slowly cooked with flavorful herbs and spices.

- **Kachamak**: is a traditional meal that is well-liked in North Macedonia's hilly areas. It is a thick porridge cooked from cornmeal and served. It often comes with cheese and sour cream (kajmak). A satisfying and soothing dish is .

- **Wine from Tikves**: The Tikves area is renowned for its wineries and vineyards. Grapes may be grown in the area because of the good soil and mild environment. Both red and white Tikves wines are well-liked and stand for the nation's winemaking legacy.

- **Prespa Carp**: also known as Prespanski Krap, is a speciality of the Prespa Lake area. Typically, this freshwater fish is breaded and fried, giving it a crunchy outside and soft inside. It often comes with a side of potatoes or salad.

- **Ajvar from Strumica**: Ajvar is a roasted red pepper condiment that is well-known across the Strumica area. Particularly renowned for its robust and smokey taste is strumica ajvar. It is a well-liked product in the area and is prepared from peppers that are cultivated nearby.

Traditional sheep husbandry is practiced in Mavrovo National Park, and the area is well-known for its premium lamb (Mavrovsko Janje). Mavrovo lamb recipes, including roasted lamb or lamb stew, showcase the meat's flavorful richness and succulent consistency.

These local delicacies provide an enjoyable gastronomic tour through North Macedonia,

139

demonstrating the variety and uniqueness of the area cuisine. Don't pass up the chance to experience these distinctive tastes while you're there.

C. Well-known eateries and cafes

There are several eateries and cafés in North Macedonia that provide delectable food and have inviting atmospheres. Here are a few well-known places to take into account:

- **The ancient Skopje Old Bazaar**: is an excellent site to learn about authentic Macedonian food. Numerous eateries and cafés may be found serving regional delicacies including Tav Grave and grilled meats.

- **Amigos Grill & Bar**: Situated in the heart of the city, Amigos is renowned for its delectable burgers, grilled foods, and laid-back ambiance. Additionally, they provide vegan and vegetarian choices.

- **Dal Met Fu**: This well-known Skopje eatery offers a fusion of Italian and Macedonian food. Their handcrafted pasta dishes and wood-fired pizzas are well regarded.

- **Public Room** : is a hip café and restaurant in Skopje that serves a varied cuisine with tastes from across the world and the Mediterranean. It's a well-liked location for food and entertainment.

- **Ohrid**: The Kaneo Restaurant, which is perched on a cliff above Lake Ohrid and provides stunning views as well as mouthwatering fresh fish and traditional Macedonian fare, is a must-try. It's the ideal location for a special meal.

- **Dr. Falafel**: In Ohrid, stop by Dr. Falafel for a fast and delectable snack. They provide delectable salads, falafel wraps, and other Middle Eastern-inspired treats.

- **The Ostrovo Restaurant**: , which is situated on the beaches of Lake Ohrid, is renowned for its laid-back ambiance and mouth watering fish specialties. It's the perfect location to eat and take in the natural splendor of the lake.

- **Restaurant Antiko**: Located in the center of Ohrid, Antiko is a family-run establishment with a warm atmosphere and a menu of traditional Macedonian specialties. The handmade sweets they provide are outstanding.

- **Bitola's Pelister Restaurant**: is a well-known eatery that offers traditional Macedonian food with a contemporary touch. There are several grilled meats, stews, and vegetarian dishes on the menu.

- **Bevanda Restaurant**: Bevanda is a well-liked option in Bitola and is renowned for both its opulent setting and a cuisine that mixes Balkan and Mediterranean tastes. A variety of seafood, grilled meats, and vegetarian options are available.

These are just a few examples of well-liked eateries and coffee shops in North Macedonia's main cities. To find hidden treasures and sample genuine Macedonian tastes, don't forget to research local recommendations and ask for advice from locals.

D. **Options for vegetarians and vegans**

North Macedonia is progressively adopting vegetarian and vegan food, and there are a number of eateries and cafés that provide these menu options. The following locations provide vegetarian and vegan food options:

- **Falafel Land**: is a Middle Eastern restaurant with a range of vegetarian and vegan alternatives, including falafel wraps, salads, and mezze platters, that is situated in the heart of Skopje.

- **Vegetarian** Kitchen : is a charming eatery in Skopje that specializes in vegetarian and vegan food produced with high-quality, regionally sourced ingredients. They provide a wide range of menu items, including pasta meals, salads, and plant-based burgers.

- **Cafe Bar Taksirat:** Taksirat is a well-liked hangout in Skopje and has distinct vegan and vegetarian menus. Along with a variety of plant-based entrees including sandwiches, wraps, and desserts, you may sip on cool drinks.

- **Ohrid**: Cafe Bar Chico: Chico is a vegetarian-friendly cafe that serves a selection of sandwiches, salads, and smoothies that are both vegetarian and vegan. Additionally, there are alternatives that are gluten-free.

The beautiful Gostilnica Kantina in Ohrid offers traditional Macedonian cuisine as well as vegetarian and vegan options. On request, they may accommodate dietary needs and offer a special vegetarian menu.

- **Kashtanot**: is a vegetarian and vegan-friendly restaurant in Bitola that specializes in organic and nutritious food. They provide a selection of salads, soups, sandwiches, and major dishes produced using ingredients acquired locally.

- **Baba Cana:** is a vegetarian-friendly restaurant that serves a fusion of Balkan and Mediterranean food. They provide alternatives for vegetarians and vegans, and are renowned for their handcrafted sweets.

Though vegetarian and vegan alternatives are expanding in North Macedonia, bear in mind that they may still be few when compared to non-vegetarian choices. However, if dietary restrictions are disclosed in advance, the majority of establishments are friendly and eager to accommodate them. You may get fresh fruits, vegetables, and other plant-based items to enjoy during your visit by exploring neighborhood markets and grocery shops.

E. Food Allergies and Restrictions

It is crucial to inform restaurant employees or lodging providers in North Macedonia of any dietary restrictions or allergies you may have. There are still possibilities even if the local food may not be as used to certain dietary requirements. Here are some pointers for dealing with food allergies and limitations in North Macedonia:

- **Express your needs**: Inform restaurant workers or hosts of your accommodations of any dietary restrictions or allergies you may have. Learning a few simple Macedonian words can help you communicate your needs clearly.

Prior to your journey, conduct some study on the common ingredients and recipes used in North Macedonian cuisine. This will assist you in locating components or allergies that you should maybe avoid.

- **Pick your traditional foods wisely**: Meat, dairy, and gluten are often included in traditional Macedonian meals. When choosing dishes, use caution and find out what ingredients were utilized. Look for recipes that are already vegetarian by nature or are more likely to meet your dietary requirements.

- **Look for vegetarian and vegan options:** Locate eateries and coffee shops that specialize in vegetarian and vegan cuisine. These places are more likely to be aware of dietary requirements and provide appropriate alternatives.

- **Bring snacks that are suitable for people with allergies**: If you have severe allergies or dietary restrictions, it's a good idea to bring some snacks that are suitable for people with allergies. This makes sure you have secure solutions available, particularly if you're going to more isolated locations.

- **Discover foreign cuisine**: You may discover a selection of international restaurants in bigger towns like Skopje that cater to a broader range of dietary needs. There are often vegetarian, vegan, and gluten-free options in Middle Eastern, Italian, and Mediterranean cuisines.

- Read the ingredient labels carefully before purchasing packaged goods or products from your neighborhood market or grocery store to be sure they don't include any allergies or components you need to avoid.

- **Speak with residents and lodging providers**: Consult the residents or the owners of your lodging for advice on where to locate appropriate restaurants. They may be able to recommend eateries or foods that fit your dietary restrictions.

To safeguard your safety, always be careful to explain your dietary requirements explicitly and double-check the components. You may negotiate dietary limitations and allergies while taking pleasure in your trip to North Macedonia with a little forward preparation and discussion.

VIII. LANGUAGE AND CULTURE

Basic Macedonian Expressions

Your ability to communicate in basic Macedonian may substantially improve your travels in North Macedonia. The following keywords will enable you to converse with locals:

* Hello: The word "zdravo"
  Happy morning: Dobro (pronounced doh-bro oo-tro)
* Happy afternoon: "Dobar den" (doh-bar den)
- Good night: Doh-brave-cher (doh-brave-cher)
* I'm grateful. Blagodaram (blah-go-dah-ram)
  Yes: Da (dah)
- No: Ne (neh)
  I'm sorry. Please, ez (eez-vee-neh-teh): The word "vi "
  Sorry: Izvinete (eez-veen-teh)
  You can speak English, right? Do you speak English? (Zbo Roo Vah Teh Ahn Glee Skee)
  I fail to comprehend: Ne razbiram, pronounced neh rahz-bee-ram

What is the price? : Kolku and meal? (koo-koo eh tseh-nah)

- Where are you: Kade e? (k-deh eh)
- Can you assist me? Are you willing to help me out? (Mo-zhe-teh Lee Dah Mee Poh Moh Nyeh Teh)
- A doctor is needed: The phrase "Mi treba doktor" (mee tre-bah dohk-tor)

  Kade e toaletot, where is the bathroom? Cheers! (kah-deh eh toh-ah-leh-toht) No problem! Noh zdrah-vyeh
- Goodbye: Voveduvanje (doh-vah-nyeh)
- Enjoy your day: Uzivajte vo (oo-zee-vah-yteh vo deh-not) Keep in mind to memorize these words and have a welcoming demeanor while speaking with natives. When traveling, even learning a few simple Macedonian words will help you establish rapport and demonstrate respect.

Cultural Customs and Etiquette

It is vital to get acquainted with the regional cultural etiquette and traditions before traveling to North Macedonia in order to have a polite and pleasurable trip. Following are some key considerations:

- **How to introduce yourself**: When meeting someone, extend a handshake and make eye contact. Use the proper greeting for the moment, such as "Dobro " (Good morning), "Dobar den" (Good afternoon), or "Dobra " (Good evening).

- **Respect for seniors**: Respect for seniors is highly regarded in Macedonian society. When speaking with elderly people, be respectful and polite.

- **Personal space**: The personal space bubble among Macedonians is usually modest. Respect this by mingling or speaking with people while keeping a safe distance.

- **Dining etiquette**: It is common to offer a little present for the host when being asked to someone's house for a dinner, such as flowers, chocolates, or a bottle of wine. Try a tiny bit of everything that is offered after waiting for the host to start eating.

North Macedonians often wear modest, conservative clothing. Cover your shoulders and knees while entering places of worship, such as monasteries or churches.

- **Politeness**: In Macedonian culture, politeness is highly regarded. When communicating with locals, use the words "please" (Vi molam) and "thank you" (Blagodaram). Until specifically asked to use their first name, it's customary to refer to them by their official title and last name.

- **Punctuality**: In North Macedonia, being on time is valued. When invited to a gathering or meeting, make an effort to show up on time or a few minutes early.

- **Religion and customs:** The religious landscape in North Macedonia is diversified. When visiting religious places, show respect and adhere to any traditions or rules that may be in place, such as taking off your shoes or covering your head.

- **Photography**: It is courteous to first seek permission before taking pictures of people, particularly natives. Recognize that some people may decline, and respect that.

- **Tipping**: Although not required, it is traditional to offer a modest tip if you are happy with the service, usually 10% of the total price.

In North Macedonia, keep in mind that distinct areas and groups may have different cultural standards. To make sure you are being courteous and thoughtful, it is usually a good idea to observe and follow local customs. Building relationships and having a more fulfilling stay in North Macedonia will be facilitated by your openness and interest in the regional traditions and customs.

Historically based arts and crafts

The traditional arts and crafts of North Macedonia have a long history and represent the workmanship and cultural variety of the nation. A fuller knowledge of North Macedonian culture may be gained by investigating these traditional crafts. Here are a some of North Macedonia's most noteworthy traditional arts and crafts:

- **Fine silver or gold wires**: are shaped and soldered to form elaborate motifs in the delicate metalworking process known as filigree. Filigree jewelry, including earrings, bracelets, and pendants with elaborate designs and themes, is popular in Skopje and Ohrid.

- **Woodcarving**: is a historic skill in North Macedonia that is often used to create ornate furniture, religious symbols, and ornamental objects. Intricately carved objects with floral, geometrical, and animal themes are produced in the city of Debar, which is especially well known for its woodcarving legacy.

- **Traditional hand-woven textiles:** including rugs, kilims, and carpets, are a beautiful example of North Macedonia's artistry and creative legacy. These fabrics include elaborate designs, vivid colors, and geometric patterns. The textile industries of Bitola and Struga are well recognized.

- **Pottery**: North Macedonia has a long history of pottery production. Plates, bowls, jugs, and figurines are just a few of the products made by talented potters that are both useful and attractive. The pottery from the city of Prilep is renowned for its earthy tones and conventional designs.

- **Embroidery**: North Macedonia has a long-standing heritage of embroidery, with each area showing its own distinctive style. Traditional textiles like tablecloths, pillows, and clothing sometimes include intricate designs and brightly colored threadwork. The needlework workmanship produced in the town of Kratovo is famous.

- **Iconography**: Iconography is important to the culture of North Macedonia because of the nation's rich religious history. Utilizing age-old methods, skilled iconographers produce stunning and profound religious artwork while creating holy icons.

- **Instruments of traditional music**: North Macedonia has a rich musical history, and traditional instruments are important to its culture. Traditional Macedonian music is often connected with the tambura, and zurla—all types of wind instruments.

You may discover these traditional arts and crafts in North Macedonia by browsing neighborhood markets, artisan stores, and cultural institutions. They provide distinctive and genuine mementos that let you bring a bit of North Macedonian culture home. Attending events like festivals, exhibits, and seminars may also give you the chance to see these crafts being made and discover more about their cultural importance.

Folk music and folklore

Traditional music and folklore are essential components of North Macedonian culture, representing the nation's rich history and many regional customs. It might be wonderful to immerse oneself in the vibrant world of North Macedonian culture and music. The following are some essential details to be aware of:

North Macedonia is home to a rich history of folk dances that are distinguished by spirited movements, deft footwork, and colorful traditional attire. The "oro," a circle dance used during festivals and festivities, is the most well-known dance form. The "teskoto oro" from Bitola or the " oro" from the Tikve area are only two examples of the distinctive dances from various places.

- **Traditional Instruments**: A key component of North Macedonian folk music is the use of traditional instruments. Traditional Macedonian music often employs the gajda (bagpipe), kaval (flute), tambura (string instrument), zurla (kind of wind instrument), and (drum).

- **Folk Songs**: "Narodni ," or North Macedonian folk songs, have a strong connection to the region's customs. These songs explore topics of ordinary life, history, nature, and love. They are often performed in Macedonian or regional dialects and accompanied by traditional instruments.

- **Folk Festivals**: All around North Macedonia, a number of folk festivals are held each year to celebrate the rich folklore and traditional music of the region. Folk dances, music, and traditional melodies are performed during two renowned cultural events, the Ohrid Summer Festival and the Struga Poetry Evenings.

- **Traditional Dress**: Each area in North Macedonia has its own distinctive traditional dress that reflects the local way of life. These elaborately created outfits include hand-woven fabrics, bright embroidery, and ornamental features. The elegance of these traditional clothes is often highlighted at festivals and cultural events.

- **Folk Ensembles**: Also referred to as "," folk ensembles are made up of musicians, singers, and dancers that specialize in preserving and presenting traditional Macedonian music and dance. These groups are vital to preserving and spreading the nation's folklore for next generations.

You may get a real sense of North Macedonian culture and traditional music through participating in folk festivals, touring cultural institutions, and discovering local music scenes. You may take in exciting performances, participate in customary dances, and become lost in the entrancing rhythms and melodies of this vivid cultural legacy.

IX. HEALTH AND SAFETY

Emergency Phone Numbers

When visiting North Macedonia, having access to emergency contacts is crucial. The following are some crucial emergency numbers to remember:

- **Officers: 192**

In the event of an emergency, an accident, or any criminal occurrence needing quick help, call the police.
194 ambulance

For medical emergencies or if someone needs immediate medical care, call this number to order an ambulance.

- **Fire Department: 193**

Contact the fire department for help if there is a fire or other emergency.

- **Service for Mountain Rescue: 112**

If you need rescue or help when engaging in outdoor activities in a hilly location, call emergency services at (112) and ask for the Mountain Rescue Service.

- **Police for Travelers: +389 2 3092 660**

The Tourist Police provide support and information designed especially for travelers. They may assist with any travel-related problems, such as reporting theft, getting lost, or asking basic questions.

- **Emergency number in general: 112**

Any emergency in North Macedonia should be reported by calling this general emergency number. Depending on your circumstances, it links you to the right emergency agency.

It's a good idea to save these phone numbers in your contacts or have them nearby for easy access. Be careful to further acquaint yourself with the unique emergency protocols and contact details offered by your lodging or local authorities.

Medical Services and Facilities

It's essential to be informed of the medical services and facilities in North Macedonia before visiting there in case you have any medical problems or crises. Here is some detail about medical services and facilities in North Macedonia:

- **Hospitals**: There are several hospitals and medical facilities spread all over North Macedonia. The following are a some of the prominent hospitals in Skopje, the nation's capital:

(Klinicki Centar Skopje) Clinical Center
Mother Teresa University Hospital Center at
Acibadem Sistina Hospital

- **Pharmacies**: In North Macedonia, pharmacies are referred to as "атека" () and may be found in towns and cities. They often provide an extensive selection of both prescription and over-the-counter medicines. To find a pharmacy, look for the sign with the green cross.

- **Travel insurance:** It is strongly advised to obtain all-inclusive travel insurance that pays for medical costs, including hospitalization, emergency care, and medical evacuation. Carry a copy of your insurance policy and the numbers for an emergency contact.

- **English-speaking physicians**: You may discover physicians and medical experts at popular tourist destinations and large cities. If necessary, these professionals may provide medical advice and support. Inquire about suggestions from the people who live nearby or at your accommodation.

- **vaccines**: It is essential to speak with your doctor or a travel clinic before heading to North Macedonia to learn about any required vaccines or health precautions for the area.

It's crucial to keep in mind that various parts of North Macedonia may provide healthcare services and facilities of varying quality and accessibility. Call the local emergency number (194) to request an ambulance or get to the closest hospital in the event of a medical emergency. You may visit a neighborhood clinic for non-emergency medical difficulties or get information about nearby medical services from your lodging by getting in touch with them.

When seeking medical attention, don't forget to bring any essential prescription prescriptions, identification papers, and insurance information. When visiting a new nation, it is usually preferable to be organized and knowledgeable about the medical facilities and services that are offered there.

Health precautions and vaccination

To guarantee a safe and healthy visit, it's crucial to take any essential vaccinations and health measures into account while planning a trip to North Macedonia. To remember, have the following in mind:

- **Ensure that you are currently on normal vaccines:** such those for influenza, measles, mumps, and rubella (MMR), diphtheria, tetanus, and pertussis (DTaP), and varicella (chickenpox).

- **Hepatitis A and B vaccinations:** are advised for visitors to North Macedonia, particularly if they want to interact closely with the locals, consume traditional cuisine, or travel through remote regions.

- **Consider being vaccinated against rabies:** if you anticipate being around animals or spending time in rural locations. It's always best to stay away from stray animals.

- **Tick-Borne Encephalitis**: If you want to spend a lot of time outside, especially in wooded areas, you might think about being immunized against tick-borne encephalitis, which is spread by tick bites.

- **Mosquito-Borne illnesses:** Although North Macedonia normally has a minimal risk of mosquito-borne illnesses, it is nevertheless essential to take protection against mosquito bites. Wear protective clothes, bug repellents, and sleep in screened-in or air-conditioned rooms.

- **Food and Water Safety**: Tap water is usually regarded as being safe to consume in North Macedonia's main cities. But it's better to stick to bottled water if you're uncertain. Use proper cleanliness while handling food, choose completely cooked meals, and choose fruits that can be peeled.

- **Traveler's diarrhea:** It is advised to maintain excellent hand hygiene, eat only hot, well-cooked meals, stay away from raw or undercooked seafood, and peel fruits and vegetables before consuming them in order to prevent traveler's diarrhea.

It's important to speak with a medical practitioner or a travel clinic at least 4-6 weeks before your departure to discuss your unique medical requirements and get the most recent advice on vaccines and safety measures for North Macedonia.

Additionally, be sure you have sufficient travel insurance that includes emergency medical evacuation and coverage for medical costs. Carry a first aid package that includes the essentials, including medicines, bug repellent, and any prescription drugs you may need.

Your vacation to North Macedonia may be safe and fun if you follow these health advice and remain informed.

Travel Protection

When traveling to any country, including North Macedonia, it is strongly advised that you get travel insurance. In the event of unanticipated circumstances or crises while you are traveling, it offers financial protection and peace of mind. Here are some crucial considerations for travel insurance:

- Make sure your travel insurance policy covers all potential hazards associated with travel, including medical costs, emergency medical evacuation, trip cancellation or interruption, lost or delayed luggage, personal liability, and others. To understand the coverage restrictions and exclusions, thoroughly read the policy.

- Verify your travel insurance policy's medical coverage to make sure it covers emergency medical care, hospitalization, and, if necessary, medical evacuation to your home country or a nearby medical institution.

- Pre-existing issues: Let the insurance company know about any existing medical issues you may have so they can determine if they are covered. Pre-existing condition coverage or the option to buy more coverage may be available under certain plans.

- Duration and Activities: Verify that the North Macedonia portion of your vacation is fully covered by your travel insurance policy. Check your policy to see whether adventurous activities like hiking, skiing, or water sports are covered or if you need to acquire extra insurance if you want to partake in them.

- Verify that your travel insurance offers round-the-clock emergency help services. This might be useful in the event of a medical emergency, travel delays, or if you need assistance or support while traveling.

- Carry a copy of your travel insurance policy and emergency contact information with you at all times. A copy should also be given to a reliable person back home.

- Check the Details: Review your travel insurance policy's terms and conditions thoroughly, paying special attention to any deductibles, claim processes, and paperwork specifications. If the need arises, familiarize yourself with the claim-filing procedure.

- To make sure you have the proper coverage, keep in mind to be completely honest when getting travel insurance. To pick the one that best fits your requirements and budget, compare several insurance companies and plans.

An investment in travel insurance may shield you from unforeseen costs and provide crucial assistance in case of emergencies while you're visiting North Macedonia. For a worry-free and joyful travel, it is always best to be prepared and have enough insurance coverage.

X. USEFUL INFORMATION

Centers for Tourist Information

Providing information, maps, brochures, and help on different parts of your journey, tourist information centers in North Macedonia are a great resource for tourists. Important information about tourist information centers in North Macedonia may be found here:

- **Location**: Tourist information centers are often found in the nation's main cities and top tourist locations. They may be found in city centers, near tourist hotspots, railroad stations, and airports.

These facilities provide a variety of tourist assistance services, such as:

- Information about tourist attractions, famous locations, and historical places
- Travel manuals, maps, and brochures
- Recommendations for lodging, dining, and other neighborhood services
- Information about transportation, such as bus and rail timetables
- Assistance in making travel reservations and planning an itinerary
- Advice on the manners, safety measures, and regional traditions

- **Multilingual Staff**: Staff members at tourist information centers often speak English as well as other important foreign languages. They can successfully interact with guests from other countries and provide them the information and support they need.

- **Additional Services:** Some tourist information centers could provide other services like reserving tickets for cultural events, leading tours, or helping people get passes or permits for national parks or other protected places.

- **Online Resources**: A lot of tourist information centers have official websites or online portals where you may access information, download travel guides, and get in touch with them if you need help before or while on your trip.

- **Local Contacts and Recommendations:** The workers at tourist information centers may provide insightful information about the customs, culture, and undiscovered attractions of the area. They might propose less well-known locations, regional celebrations, or genuine experiences to make your vacation more memorable.

- **Hours of Operation**: Tourist information centers' hours of operation might change, although they typically adhere to normal business hours. It is essential to call ahead to confirm their business hours or ask at your lodging if there have been any alterations or closures.

To maximize your trip experience in North Macedonia, take use of the tourist information centers. Don't be afraid to contact one or go to one; they can provide you useful information and make your vacation memorable and pleasurable.

Online Resources for Travel

There are a number of online travel sites, in addition to Tourist Information Centers, that may provide helpful advice and support while organizing your trip to North Macedonia. These internet travel resources are suggested:

- Visit the official tourist website of North Macedonia for detailed information on the country's attractions, lodging options, transit options, events, and more. You may plan your route by downloading brochures, maps, and travel guides from these websites. Look up the regional tourist board or the official North Macedonia tourism website.

- Participate in travel discussion boards and online communities where you may obtain first-hand accounts, practical advice, and suggestions from other travelers who have been to North Macedonia. To interact with other travelers and get travel tips, many people use websites like TripAdvisor, Lonely Planet's Thorn Tree, and Reddit's r/travel.

- Travel websites and blogs: Many travel websites and bloggers give in-depth reports of their experiences in North Macedonia, including information on the country's tourist attractions, local customs, cuisine, and off-the-beaten-path locations. To get ideas and inspiration, look for travel blogs or websites that focus primarily on North Macedonia or the Balkans.

- Use online mapping services like Google Maps or offline maps offered by several travel applications for navigation. These might be useful before and during your journey to plan your itineraries, identify sites of interest, and navigate the streets.

- Websites of local transportation providers, such as bus or railway companies, should be checked for timetables, routes, and ticket details. You may use these websites to organize trips both inside North Macedonia and to its neighbors.

- Online booking platforms: To find and reserve rooms in North Macedonia, use trusted websites like Booking.com, Airbnb, or Agoda. These websites often include user reviews, pictures, and thorough information about the many kinds of lodgings that are offered.

- Social media: Follow North Macedonia-focused influencers, travel bloggers, and tourist boards on social media. They often provide beautiful pictures, advice on where to go, and suggestions that might make organizing your vacation easier.

- To verify accuracy and relevance, cross-reference information from several sources. Keep up to speed with the most recent travel advice, visa requirements, and safety measures offered by dependable travel providers or on official government websites.

You may learn useful information, plan your schedule, and make wise choices to have a memorable and satisfying vacation to North Macedonia by using these online travel tools.

Printed in Great Britain
by Amazon

26108491R00106